C000009855

Bach

Bach

Martin Geck

translated by Anthea Bell
introduced by John Butt

HAUS PUBLISHING · LONDON

First published in German in the Rowohlt monographien series
© 1993, 2000 Rowolht Taschenbuch Verlag GmbH

This English translation first published in Great Britain in 2003 by
Haus Publishing Limited
32 Store Street
London WC1E 7BS

English translation © Anthea Bell, 2003
Introduction © John Butt, 2003

The moral right of the authors has been asserted

A CIP catalogue record for this book
is available from the British Library

ISBN 1-904341-16-0 (paperback)
ISBN 1-904341-35-7 (hardback)

Designed and typeset in Albertina at Libanus Press, Marlborough

Printed and bound by Graphicom in Vicenza, Italy

Front cover: painting of Johann Sebastian Bach by Joachim Ernst Rentsch
courtesy of the Ann Ronan Collection
Back cover: painting of Bach courtesy of the Ann Ronan Collection

CONDITIONS OF SALE
All rights reserved. No part of this publication may be reproduced,
stored in a retrieval system, or transmitted in any form or by any
means, electronic, mechanical, photocopying, recording or
otherwise, without the prior permission of the publisher

This book is sold subject to the condition that it shall not, by way of trade
or otherwise, be lent, re-sold, hired out or otherwise circulated without
the publisher's prior consent in any form of binding or cover other than
that in which it is published and without a similar condition including
this condition being imposed on the subsequent purchaser

Contents

Introduction

Why do we want biographies of great composers? After all, there is no certainty that what we learn about their lives will tell us anything concrete about their music. At least with literary figures and visual artists we can guess, by the way they represent their imaginary worlds, something about how they have experienced their own lives. But with the medium of music there is less obviously a representational link with the outside world. None the less, we surely still hear the music of Bach and other great composers as 'representing' something – perhaps even something more immediate and tangible than 'representation' itself, as if we were experiencing the artist's emotion or sensation as it actually happened.

It is the immediacy of music, which is somehow just out of reach of our verbal descriptions, that explains our perennial fascination with the personalities of composers. We know frustratingly little about Bach's day-to-day life and character. He left so few personal letters and virtually none that could be considered truly autobiographical. Yet in recent years we have learned more about the society of his age and, of course, in some senses we know his music better than most of his contemporaries did. Even if the surviving facts are thin on the ground, there are countless ways these can be interpreted, ordered or thrown into relief by other local details. Thus, there is a considerable leeway in how a biography of Bach can be written, reflecting the openness of our interpretations of his music. Our inferences about the man and the music are somehow connected even if there is no certainty in the matter.

Despite the mystique that has grown up around Bach, for virtually every generation that discovers his music, one of the most striking things is an intangible human element, tantalisingly close yet never fully explained.

When the Bach biography became virtually a literary genre in its own right in the latter half of the 19th century, many German Lutherans evidently saw 'Bach the Man' as their saviour from the crises then facing their church. He was recast as the 'fifth Evangelist', who had been the living embodiment of the intense religious faith and 'real presence' that his music seemed to transmit. Both the music and the man seemed to share a moral and spiritual perfection, that offered an escape from an alienating age of modernisation and secularisation. Thus, Bach was a precious reminder of 'Lost Eden' where music, man and the cosmos resonated perfectly together under the harmonious grace of God.

This view of Bach as a supremely religious figure was largely cast aside in the mid-20th century, when scholars undertook a dispassionate, quasi-scientific examination of Bach's surviving manuscripts. This revealed that Bach wrote most of his Leipzig church music during the first five years of his appointment, thereafter turning to other things, merely recycling his cantatas in yearly cycles. Perhaps he wrote church music only because it was his duty to his employers, and was otherwise mainly concerned with the advancement of his compositional and social status. After all, in an age when it was virtually impossible *not* to be religious, how could one particular person be proven more religious than the rest? The mid-20th century was also a time when many viewed music as isolated from the rest of the world and laid great store in the autonomous ingenuity of the musical structure. Bach's music had thus become a model for many of the great modern composers – in particular, Stravinsky and Schoenberg – the high modernists saw his music as an entity separate from the uncertainties and imperfections of human embodiment. To many then, a biography of Bach would have been seen as a Romantic irrelevance, merely something for those unable to appreciate the structural complexity of 'the music itself'. It was in the autonomous, self-reflexive musical material that the 'truth' could be found; anything beyond this was merely vague speculation, relying on feeble human emotions and imaginative fiction.

The last decade of the 20th century, leading up to the year 2000 (the 250th anniversary of Bach's death), saw a vigorous return to Bach biography. Many of us had certainly felt that something was lacking in writing on Bach: scholarly work either concentrated entirely on the structural nature of the music in an entirely 'objective' way, or it centred on the forensic study of the original sources that eschewed anything that could not directly be 'proven'. One question that could well have been asked was: 'Why did we value Bach's music in the first place?' Much existing writing seemed to assume that Bach's music was uniformly great, as if it were a religious text whose truth could not be questioned. Yet in the wider world of musical culture there was a tremendous amount of debate about the relative value of many different types of music; as an institution, even 'classical music' itself was coming under siege in an increasingly pluralistic society. Conversely, many were once again clearly seeking solace in Bach's music in an unashamedly religious manner. How can Bach's music, written by a composer born over 300 years ago, still have any relevance for our concerns? Some form of historical perspective suddenly seems very important again.

Yet even here there is no obvious strategy to adopt: should our biographies emphasise the similarities between Bach's age and ours, as if to explain why so much seems familiar about his music? Or should our biographies show the remarkable differences between the two eras – this could, after all, make the modern-day success of his music seem even more remarkable? Another factor for consideration could be how Bach's music has been regarded in the intervening years, between his age and ours; those years – often ignored in

INTRODUCTION

most Bach scholarship, might, after all, have shaped many of our own conceptions. Indeed Bach's music has surely influenced many of the great composers of the classical tradition, and is thus present as a background against which many works can be heard. In this context, then, a biography would help us filter out those elements of Bach appreciation that have been constant from those that have developed over the following centuries, partly through the composition of new music. We would then be able to trace something of the genealogy of our own cultural position.

What renders Martin Geck such a perceptive scholar of Bach is his remarkably deep knowledge of how the composer 'was rediscovered' during the opening decades of the 19th century. His sense of how the music became separated from the composer and was subsequently reintegrated into new stories of the composer's personality is particularly acute.

One idea that immediately emerges from his biography is that Bach's relatively provincial Eisenach background was something that he never fully relinquished. In other words, he plumbed the greatest depth of experience from a relatively modest environment. Ironically, this gave his music much value in later centuries. Had this music been truly fashionable or cosmopolitan in its own age, overfilled with local relevance, it would surely have sounded dated in later years. But Bach's strikingly profound exploration of a limited world somehow translates well to subsequent eras. The historical material is relatively easily assimilated by any to whom it is alien, yet Bach's treatment of it is the most penetrating and challenging imaginable.

Another point that rendered him such a 'hardy traveller' in later ages is that he did not cultivate a deliberately idiosyncratic personality. This biography shows us that his principal means of learning was the traditional one: study and improving exemplars. As Geck observes, Bach spent many years working on the same few works, and the exact beginning and ending of the process cannot (and should not) necessarily be traced. It is as if the composer is aiming for a perfection that is not humanly achievable. The very openness of these works, coupled with their intense perfection, somehow gives them a momentum that carries them into the future.

Idiosyncratic his compositional personality may not have been, but there is no doubt that Bach's personality was extremely strong. Geck reveals an extravagant, 'virtuoso' character in Bach's fiery encounters with the council of Arnstadt. As a virtuoso, Bach seems to wish to say as much as possible all in one moment, and this develops into a more mature dialectic, between the cultivation of the greatest intensity of expression and the greatest degree of order in his music. Geck discerns Bach's search for ultimate truth in his basic compositional philosophy of 'all-in-one' and 'all-from-one' (his deriving of the entire composition from as small a number of elements as possible). Once again, this relates to Bach's development of the most intense musical vision from a straitened environment.

Did Bach thus cultivate a sense of individuality, a sense of autonomous art, within the context of what was basically a traditional craft-like activity? Geck suggests that there was a real sense in which Bach's music performed a covert social function somehow sublimating, his professional problems and the various contradictions of his age, such as between church and art. In this way, Bach's music does indeed relate to the German tradition of the following century, not least the art of Beethoven, which similarly articulates a special kind of humanity by transcending the difficulties of life.

Geck is not afraid to ask searching, critical questions of Bach's music. He notes that some cantatas might well have been composed in his sleep, and certain arias run on 'automatic pilot'. He finds the *Italian Concerto* rather mechanical and vapid, perhaps because this was one of the pieces that Bach's most noted critic, J A Scheibe, actually liked. This brings up the question of whether music should follow the gestalt form of figure/ground, as is the norm in popular music and art (as also championed by Scheibe), or whether it should combine three or more equal parts in a more challenging and sophisticated form of art, as tended to be Bach's preference.

This, of course, relates very strongly to debates that are still current today, as an increasingly pluralistic culture not only tends to sponsor the simpler, popular options but also demands that the virtues of each art form be more explicitly justified. What Geck is so eloquent in revealing about Bach is the fact that our appreciation of this music works on so many levels. This leads him to view issues such as number symbolism as red herrings that divert us from the real nourishment that we derive from this most subtle of musics.

So what do we learn of Bach's personality from this fascinating counterpoint of music and biographical detail? The composer seems to have enjoyed the richest foods, to have consorted with colourful Leipzig personalities, such as would have been found at the regular meetings of the *Collegium Musicum*. Geck concludes that, as a man, Bach was probably opinionated and quick tempered, but also sociable and humorous. As a composer, he could be compared with Faust, desiring to know what really holds the world together, standing between medieval, alchemic world-views and modernity. If some find Geck's specifically German perspective far-fetched – such as seeing Bach as a universal figure, seeking what is perfect and quintessential in the company of Beethoven, Brahms and the Second Viennese school – at the very least, we have an image of Bach that goes beyond the merely documentary or adulatory. Geck's taut web linking music, man, context and historical process gains a quality not unlike Bach's art: we can take it or leave it, but cannot fail to be impressed.

John Butt
Gardiner Professor of Music
University of Glasgow
Editor, *Cambridge Companion to Bach*

The early years: youth and early experiences as an organist
1685–1708

The character of Johann Sebastian Bach illustrates the futility of wondering whether musical talent is innate or acquired. Generations of his family tree consist of musicians and nothing but musicians. Do we, therefore, conclude that the Bachs had a special musical gene? Or was it the atmosphere around little Johann Sebastian, pervaded as it was by music, that told him from the moment he first drew breath: you will survive, flourish and win fame in this climate only as a musician?

Neither notion answers satisfactorily the question of the nature of Bach's artistic genius. Why can some people not only command a certain aspect of human experience more capably and indeed passionately than others, but in doing so show an apparently natural ability to touch upon nerve centres common to many people through the ages?

Bach's paternal lineage can be traced back uninterruptedly to the 16th century. The patriarch is considered to be Veit (Vitus) Bach, who had to flee from Hungary about 1545 at a time when protestants were being persecuted, and who set up as a baker in his new home at Wechmar near Gotha.

If Veit Bach contented himself, as he ground grain into flour, with plucking the *Cithrinchen* (little cittern), a popular folk instrument, his son Johannes, who took over the bakery in spite of having a good musical education, was a part-time *Spielmann* (minstrel player) who helped out with musical performances from time to time. Music was the principal profession of his own sons Johann, Christoph

Bach's father: Johann Ambrosius Bach (1645–95), director of the Eisenach town music ensemble. Painting by Johann David Herlicius, 1685

and Heinrich. The eldest became a member of the town musical ensemble in Erfurt, while the two younger sons went to Arnstadt a few years later as organists and town musicians.

Some sacred vocal and organ music by Johann and Heinrich Bach is extant, but none by Christoph Bach, who himself had three sons, including the twins Johann Christoph and Johann Ambrosius, born in 1645. Johann Christoph lived in Arnstadt as a court and town musician. Johann Ambrosius also began his career in Arnstadt but then became a town musician in Erfurt, and was later court trumpeter and director of the Eisenach town ensemble.

While he was still in Erfurt, Johann Ambrosius Bach married Elisabeth Lämmerhirt, the daughter of a furrier of high standing in the town. Elisabeth bore him six sons and two daughters. Johann Sebastian was the youngest child, born on 21 March 1685 and baptised two days later in St George's church in Eisenach, with the musician Sebastian Nagel of Gotha and the forester Johann Georg Koch of Eisenach as his godfathers. The 'Bach House' on the Frauenplan in Eisenach – today a Bach museum that attracts many visitors – can no longer be considered Bach's actual birthplace, which was probably a building on the site of what is now 35 Lutherstrasse.

The history of Johann Sebastian Bach's siblings can be traced only in part. We shall encounter his oldest brother to survive, the organist Johann Christoph, during Bach's Ohrdruf period. The brother nearest to Johann Sebastian in age was Johann Jakob, a musician in Swedish service. Marie Salome married and went to live in Erfurt.

Entry recording Bach's baptism. Register of St George's church, Eisenach, 23 March 1685

Johann Rudolf, Johann Balthasar, Johann Jonas and Johanna Juditha did not survive to adulthood.

The extended family included composers of some significance, but there is no room for a detailed account of them here. Johann Sebastian Bach copied out some of their works and performed them himself. These pieces included compositions by the two Eisenach organists Johann Christoph and Johann Bernhard, by Johann Nikolaus, organist of Jena, and Johann Ludwig, court Kapellmeister in Meiningen. It says much for Johann Sebastian's sense of tradition and family feeling that in 1735, he compiled an account of the *Ursprung der musicalisch-Bachischen Familie* (Origin of the Musical Bach Family)[1] with brief biographies of 53 family members; without that chronicle, the *Genealogy*, we would have much less information about the family tree.

It seems like a special dispensation of Providence that Bach happened to be born in Eisenach, which had a population of about 6,000 at the time, and lived there until he was 11. As if in a miniature model, the town offered the boy everything that would make up the man's life over the following decades: his parental home, which served as headquarters of the *Stadtpfeiferei* or town musical ensemble, and where apprentices and journeymen also lived; the Latin School, with a long tradition behind it, situated in the old Dominican monastery; the principal town church of St George with its organ and a choir capable of performing polyphonic music; the town hall with its wind band for playing 'tower pieces' (performed from the

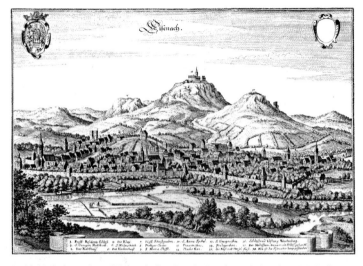

Bach's birthplace: view of Eisenach showing the Wartburg, in Matthäus Merian's *Topographia* of 1650

balcony of the town hall); the *Kurrende* (poor schoolboys who sang for alms); and finally the nearby Wartburg, seat of the ruling Duke of Saxony-Eisenach, where performances of courtly suites, concerti, sonatas and cantatas were given.

If looked at it in this light, Bach never broke away from the 'primal scene' of his Eisenach childhood, but merely built productively on it in his later career. He remained in the Thuringian and Saxon area, and his travels never took him further from home than Hamburg, Lübeck and Berlin in the north, Karlsbad (Karlovy Vary) in the south and Kassel in the west.

Bach's professional life is a sharp contrast to that of George Frideric Handel, his contemporary and opposite number, who was born into a prosperous family of the middle or almost upper-middle class only a few weeks earlier in Halle, not very far away. From the first, Handel was drawn to travel: to Hamburg for the great experiment in 'German opera'; to Italy to study and practise modern music at its source; and to England, where he became a great national figure and his mortal remains were laid to rest in Westminster Abbey.

Bach, on the other hand, reminds one more of the young Martin Luther, who exactly two centuries earlier had himself attended the Latin school where Bach studied from 1693 to 1695. Neither Bach nor Luther, who had to sing for alms with the *Kurrende* outside the houses and tombs of the citizens of Eisenach, was a stranger to poverty, and even in his youth, or at least from the time when he was orphaned, Bach must have known that his life was to be one of work and study. His mother and father died within nine months of each other, in 1694 and 1695 respectively.

Johann Sebastian and Johann Jakob were left in the care of Johann Christoph, their eldest brother, who had become organist at the church of St Michael in Ohrdruf, halfway between Eisenach and Arnstadt. What would the ten year old have remembered from his childhood in Eisenach? The sounds of trumpet and violin, spinet and organ ringing in his ears from morning to night may well have introduced him to the infinite world of musical sound; the basic school subjects of Latin, Holy Scripture and choral singing will have conveyed some idea of what his later profession as Kantor would entail; and his father's duties in church, in the town and at court, determined as they were by guild and social constructs, must have given him some premonition of the subservience and everyday drudgery that went with such a career.

Bach's first hymnbook: beginning of the 'Passion' section in the Eisenach hymnbook of 1673. Such emblematic depictions informed Bach's understanding of God and the world, and found their counterpart in the figurative and symbolic quality of his music.

Johann Christoph Bach (1642–1703), the cousin of Bach's father and probably his teacher. He was organist at Eisenach, and chamber musician at the court of Eisenach. He composed music, and may have introduced the young Johann Sebastian to composition. Anonymous painting, c.1700

Perhaps Bach had also received some incidental instruction in playing the violin from his father, and an introduction to the art of composition from his father's cousin Johann Christoph, who lived locally and was a composer of some importance.

However, his real musical training seems to have begun in Ohrdruf. A smaller place than Eisenach, Ohrdruf none the less offered Johann Sebastian plenty of opportunities for education and musical training. There was a highly regarded school, the Lyceum, where pupils were prepared in the *prima* (top class) for admission to university if they were still studying Latin and Greek. The principal church of St Michael had a *chorus musicus* performing motets and concerted sacred music on Sundays and for church festivals. And Ohrdruf was the home of Bach's brother Johann Christoph, 14 years his senior, who had just set up his own household there.

The orphan's living conditions cannot have been very luxurious: his brother's income was small and the family's accommodation cramped. Young Bach will have been glad to get a free place at the Lyceum as a *Kurrende* singer, although that meant performing many arduous duties after school in summer and winter alike, even while he was quite young. The same life would have fallen to the lot of his brother Johann Jakob, three years older than Johann Sebastian, but before the end of 1695, Johann Jakob had returned to his birthplace and taken up an apprenticeship as town musician with his father's successor in Eisenach. A few years later, as a military musician in the service of Sweden, he was travelling the battlefields of Europe as far afield as Turkey, and he then settled down for life in Stockholm as a member of the Swedish court Kapelle.

Johann Sebastian was still too young to be able to think of such independence, or indeed such freedom from ties. In any case, he seems to have been a different kind of character: someone intent on forging a successful career within the social and intellectual milieu where he was placed, so that later he could draw on the opportunities it offered and, as an artist, break its mould, although without abandoning it. As a result, he studied hard at the Lyceum, was top of the class at first, and was always among the best pupils.

However, the musical studies with his brother on which he eagerly began must have mattered to him more. Johann Christoph, according to the article on Bach in Johann Gottfried Walther's *Musicalisches Lexicon* of 1732, taught him 'the first *principia* on the clavier'; in the linguistic usage of the time this will have included the organ.

What kind of teaching was given to a boy who had already gone beyond the very first beginner's stages? Bach must have learnt from *exempla*, that is pieces that his brother had written down in his manuscript books of musical notation in order to play from them himself. Printed music was a rarity at the time; a good organist compiled his own repertory. And Johann Sebastian's elder brother was indeed a good organist: his father had known what he was doing when he sent him to Erfurt to study with the famous Johann Pachelbel for three years.

As his skills increased, Johann Sebastian probably learned much of Pachelbel's music by heart, transcribed it and perhaps transferred such works as preludes, fugues, fugal chorale preludes and keyboard suites to a music book of his own. But we may assume that his interest already went beyond these limited horizons. A contemporaneous copy of Dietrich Buxtehude's *Prelude and Fugue in G minor* (Buxtehude-WV 148) is in two hands, one the handwriting

7

of Johann Christoph Bach, the other that of an apparently younger copyist.[2] It is tempting to imagine Johann Sebastian gaining an insight into north German organ music as he helped his brother to copy the work.

Was he perhaps so eager to get to know new works that his brother felt he had to restrain him on occasion and insist on his own prior rights? The touching story in the *Nekrolog* (*Obituary*, written by Bach's son Carl Philipp Emanuel (C P E) Bach and J F Agricola, and first published in 1754)[3] may not be entirely imaginary: we are told that the younger brother went to a cupboard with grille-work doors, that contained a book of pieces by the keyboard masters Johann Jakob Froberger, Johann Kaspar Kerll and Johann Pachelbel that his elder brother did not want him to have yet. His hands were small enough for him to reach through the grillework, roll up the book and take it out, and he strained his eyes to copy the music by moonlight.

Although this anecdote may be embroidering upon what was really a minor incident, it does cast light on an important feature of Bach's character, one that emerged again and again in later life: his passion, indeed obsession, with conquering the realm of music and making it entirely his own. Some want to learn a craft, others wish for fame – Bach's ambition was to be the complete master of his art.

Bach's first home away from his native town: view of Ohrdruf, where he went in 1695 to live with his elder brother Johann Christoph (1671–1721) after the death of his parents. Anonymous engraving

As children began to be born to his brother, the family home must have seemed increasingly crowded, and free places for pupils at the Ohrdruf Lyceum were few and far between. It was fortunate, therefore, that when Bach had celebrated his 15th birthday, he was recommended by the new Kantor of the Lyceum to St Michael's monastery in Lüneburg, which not only required 'Matins singers' but could offer them free schooling. Travelling on foot in the time-honoured manner of the wayfaring journeyman, probably in the company of his classmate Georg Erdmann, Bach set off for Lüneburg, where they arrived before Easter of 1700.

Strictly speaking, the monastery of St Michael was not a monastery at all, nor had it been for some time; instead, it was a well-endowed foundation comprising the church, a boarding-school for the sons of noblemen known as the *Ritterakademie*, the Latin School for middle-class boys and the *Collegium Academicum*, an establishment similar to a university. According to the statutes, stipends were provided for about 12 boys and some older choristers to sing in the 'Matins choir' at Matins and Vespers – they had once been known as 'the poor singing scholars'. Naturally, Bach did not take part just in the minor church services but also sang in the 'chorus symphoniacus' providing music for the principal services on Sundays and church festivals. As his voice soon broke, however, his activities, assuming that he did not instantly develop a mature male voice, must have extended to other duties – perhaps those of assistant organist.

The opportunities for study open to Bach in Lüneburg were good. The music library of St Michael's was one of the largest anywhere in Germany at a time when music was handed down mainly in manuscript. Bach could become familiar with the whole tradition of the evangelical sacred

The scene of Bach's first employment: St Michael's church in Lüneburg. As a scholarship boy, from 1700 onwards, Bach sang polyphonic music in the choir and thus became acquainted with major works of north German sacred music. Painting by Joachim Burmester, *c.*1700

9   SCHOLARSHIP BOY

music of the 16th and 17th centuries here; even if he was thought too young for such theoretical study, he must at least have gained practical insight into the ecclesiastical musical culture of north Germany through his participation in the performances of motets, sacred concerted music and cantatas on Sundays, and church festivals in St Michael's.

He will also have become acquainted with the organ repertory. Lüneburg had two outstanding organists at this time: Georg Böhm and Johann Jakob Löwe. It is true that there is no evidence of Bach taking organ lessons from either of them, but the idea cannot be ruled out entirely, for the *Obituary* mentioned above gives an account of the young Matins singer's much more extravagant activities: 'From Lüneburg he journeyed now and again to Hamburg, to hear the then famous Organist of the Catharinen-Kirche, Johann Adam Reinken. And here, too, he had the opportunity to go and listen to a then famous band kept by the Duke of Zelle, and consisting for the most part of Frenchmen; thus, he acquired a thorough grounding in the French taste.'[4]

Bach did not necessarily have to visit neighbouring Celle to study the 'French taste', since the court Kapelle sometimes played in Lüneburg, and one of its members would stay under the same roof as him. This was Thomas Selle, violinist and dancing master of the *Ritterakademie*, which in view of its pupils' rank set less store by humanist studies than instruction in French conversation, the art of dancing, and 'the writing of elegant letters'.[5]

Though Bach may not have visited the German opera company (founded in Hamburg in 1678) when he travelled to that city, during his Lüneburg years he had the chance to study musical life in great variety, with the exception of Italian music, for Bach's formative experiences in that area of modern music did not come until later, in Weimar. It is not known which of the opportunities Bach actually took up; it can only be certain that in one way or another he transformed himself into an outstanding organist and an authority on the instrument. How else could he have acquitted himself so brilliantly as an organist in Arnstadt just a few years later?

Hungry, but too poor to eat at an inn, Bach picked up discarded fish heads in an alleyway on his way back from Hamburg to Lüneburg. Low and behold: he found a Danish ducat hidden in each head.

From *Legends of the Music Saints* by Friedrich Wilhelm Marpurg, 1786

However, more is known about his school work. When Bach was accepted into the *prima* class in Lüneburg, the following subjects were on the syllabus: Latin, including grammar and the reading of Cicero's orations against Catiline and Virgil's *Aeneid*; Greek, focusing on the translation of the New Testament; theology, studied from Leonhard Hutter's strictly orthodox *Compendium locorum theologicorum*; logic from Andreas Reyher's *Systema Logicum*; rhetoric from a compendium by Heinrich Tolle; and philosophy and versification.[6]

However, there can be no doubt that these foundations of humanist and theological ideas, laid at the Ohrdruf and Lüneburg Latin Schools, allowed Bach to become a 'learned composer' (*musicus doctus*) even though he had never been to university. The term 'learned composer' denoted a musician with traditional training, respectful of the old values. With such a grounding, he could hold his own among any of his contemporaries, some of whom had a different if not necessarily less good training, and here, in his later life, he swam against the current of the time.

Bach graduated from St Michael's in Easter, 1702, aged 17. In the second half of that year he applied unsuccessfully for the post of organist at St Jacobi's church in Sangerhausen, and from March to September 1703 he is entered as a 'lackey', most probably a violinist, in the salary register of the joint ruler of Saxe-Weimar, Duke Johann Ernst.

That autumn Bach inspected a new organ, maybe for the first time in his life but certainly not for the last. He was paid 4 thalers for his report on the instrument in the *Neukirche* in Arnstadt, which had

Bach was a famous judge of organs. Johann Nicolaus Forkel recounts how Bach inspected the instruments. He first played the piece in its entirety to see *if the organ had a good lung*, then inspected the instrument's individual parts. To conclude his evaluation, Bach gave a short concert, which was often followed by a feast.

a double manual and 23 stops. This was rather unusual, but no doubt the activities of so many other distinguished members of the Bach family lent gravitas to the young man's name in this small town of about 3,800 inhabitants on the outskirts of the Thuringian Forest. We may also assume that when he reported on the organ it was probably already agreed that Johann Sebastian himself would be playing it officially from the next month. None the less, at 18 he was extraordinarily young to deliver such a report. Whatever the circumstances, Bach embarked on a career which, as the *Obituary* puts it, would make him 'the greatest organist and clavier player that we have ever had',[7] and in the opinion of many of his contemporaries the greatest organ authority in Europe.

Bach's first post was a modest one, as the *Neukirche* was the least important of the three churches in Arnstadt. As far as the performance of vocal works was concerned it had to survive, musically speaking, on the scraps that fell from the tables of the other churches. But for the first time in his life Bach had some free time. As organist, he had to play only for the main service on Sundays and church festivals, the Monday prayer service, Vespers on Wednesdays and early Thursday service, and to perform (with the requisite modifications) a prelude and postlude, chorale prelude and chorale accompaniment, and a voluntary- or a chorale-based work during communion. Whether he

The springboard of Bach's career: Arnstadt. Engraving by Pius Rösel von Rosenhoff, c.1700, after Meister Wolf, c.1570

was also to deputise for the Kantor and direct small-scale vocal performances with the few pupils available to him was a point at issue with the consistory, his ecclesiastical authority.

Bach used his release from the strictly regulated life of his school-days, when he probably never had a spare moment, to study intensively on his own; there is no other way of explaining his rapid development as a composer. It comes as no surprise to find Carl Philipp Emanuel writing of his father that 'through his own study and reflection alone he became even in his youth a pure and strong fugue writer'.[8] He was anything but a stay-at-home constantly poring over his music, but made good use of his social and artistic opportunities. He wore a sword in the street perhaps emulating the pupils at the Lüneburg *Ritterakademie* – and one evening made as if to draw in self-defence against a student called Geyersbach. Previously, he had criticised this man as a *fool of a bassoon-ist*, making this the particular occasion for airing his general annoyance at being given only unqualified students to help him perform vocal music. Unusually for the time, he preferred to have *a young woman who was a stranger to the town* singing for him in the organ loft.

Bernd Göbel's beautiful bronze statue of the young Bach in a self-confident posture has stood in the market square of Arnstadt since 1985. Göbel portrays the young Bach as already displaying the assurance of a man who knew the breadth of his capabilities.

On several occasions, Bach was called to account for such untowardness to the consistory, which also accused him of taking unauthorised leaves of absence and irritating the congregation with his elaborate organ playing. The minutes of one such consistorial meeting follow:

'*Actum*, February 21, 1706

The Organist in the *Neukirche*, Bach, is interrogated as to where he has lately been for so long and from whom he obtained leave to go.

Ille [he]: He has been to Lübeck in order to comprehend one thing and another about his art, but had asked leave

CONSISTORY

beforehand by the superintendent.

Dominus Superintendens [Superintendent]: He had asked for only four weeks, but had stayed about four times as long.

Ille: Hoped that the organ playing had been so taken care of by the one he had engaged for the purpose that no complaint could be entered on that account.

Nos [we]: Reprove him for having hitherto made many curious *variationes* in the chorale, and mingled many strange tones in it, and for the fact that the congregation has been confused by it. In the future, if he wished to introduce a *tonus peregrinus* [a remote key], he was to hold it out, and not to turn too quickly to something else, or, as had hitherto been his habit, even play a *tonus contrarius* [a dissonance]. In addition, it was quite disagreeable that hitherto no instrumental music had been performed, for which he was responsible . . .

The student, Rambach: The organist Bach had previously played rather too long, but after his attention had been called to it by the Superintendent, he had at once fallen into the other extreme and had made it too short.'[9]

This is quite a list of accusations. Indeed, Bach was still not getting the students to perform instrumental music; instead, he had been away in Lübeck for four months and not the agreed four weeks, 'in order to listen to the famous Organist at the Marein-Kirche there, Dietrich Buxtehude', as the *Obituary* tells us.[10]

Having been reprimanded in general for playing too long on the organ, Bach defiantly cut the performance too short. Nor was that all: in words the meaning of which is not entirely clear, although they sound knowledgeable, the consistory pointed out that Bach was accompanying the congregational hymn in an over-elaborate rather than a moderate manner. They had a point: Bach's harmonisation of the hymn *Herr Jesu Christ, dich zu uns wend (Lord Jesus Christ, turn thou to us)* in the organ chorale BWV 726, very probably of this period, might well serve to illustrate the consistory's complaints:

Two important role models and teachers: Johann Adam Reinken (at the harpsichord) and Dietrich Buxtehude (with head propped on his hand; not identified beyond all doubt). Although it is a stylised genre piece, this scene of music-making, painted in 1674 by Johannes Voorhout, is evidence of the high social status accorded in the Hanseatic area to the art of solo vocal, organ and chamber music, particularly as practised by north German organists.

in this setting, Bach plays with labyrinthine chromatic possibilities of a four-part setting in a way that distracts attention from the cantus firmus rather than illuminating it.

The hot-headed young Bach had his own interpretation of the old maxim *Non hominibus, sed deo* (Not unto men but unto God), placed by his new teacher Buxtehude at the head of one of his learned canons: he saw his calling as not being to serve an apathetic congregation or reactionary authorities, but to make the highest possible use of his art.

Barely 20, he was not to be deterred from staying in Lübeck by the risk of losing his post, and would not make the walk home again before attending the famous *Abendmusiken* (musical recitals) given in that town, which unfortunately took place only once a year during Advent.

Bach made the fullest use of the freedom of movement that

The work of the most interesting German composer between Schütz and Bach, Dietrich Buxtehude (1673–1707), illustrates a change in musical and social history similar to that which had taken place in Italy a century earlier: church music emancipated itself from pure service to the Scriptural text and the liturgy and aimed for directly sensuous effect. Bach's creative work is linked to the endeavour to merge these new, anthropocentric musical ideas with the traditional theocentric attitude, forming a higher unity.

he now considered to be his. Having mainly studied the organ masters of central and southern Germany in Ohrdruf, and despite what he may have heard and learnt in Lüneburg and Hamburg, he was increasingly drawn to Buxtehude as the greatest master of the north German organ style. Within three months he had not only learnt everything Buxtehude (who at nearly 70 was a very old man for those days) could teach him about the organ, but also studied his vocal music, from the sensitive early Pietist solo cantata to the magnificent musical recitals for large forces 'with all the choirs and organs'.

Bach's visit to Lübeck was made to study Buxtehude not just as a composer but also as a virtuoso. It was his organ music that stood or fell according to the performer's skill in exploiting the specific tonal possibilities of the north German organ in volume, variety of solo stops and pedal strength. This factor in Bach's life was over-estimated by his contemporaries and his sons, but later biographers tended to undervalue it. At first Bach aspired more to the career of a keyboard and organ virtuoso, writing his own pieces for perfor-

The organ and the harpsichord were the most important instruments for a keyboard virtuoso. Certain pieces, however – the *Well-tempered Clavier*, for example – sound best on the clavichord. Because it was a more affordable instrument than the harpsichord, the clavichord was also used for home entertainment and practice.

mance, than to that of a 'learned composer' (*musicus doctus*) of his later years. After his appointment as Konzertmeister at Weimar these aspects coincided, but while he was still in Köthen Bach saw himself primarily as a keyboard master. Only in Leipzig did his image as a *musicus doctus* gradually become dominant. The extravagance of Bach's organ performances in Arnstadt was more than mere youthful impetuosity: he was laying the foundations of a virtuoso career.

A man with Bach's energetic disposition could not be expected to stay very long in one place. In fact, he was 22 when he auditioned on the organ in the church of St Blasius at Mühlhausen in Thuringia. On 14 June he put his conditions to the responsible church authorities: he wanted the same salary as he had received in Arnstadt plus the payments in kind that had gone to his predecessor, whose salary had actually been lower. He was appointed to the post the next day.

On 17 October, he married his cousin Maria Barbara Bach, six months his senior, at Dornheim near Arnstadt. Maria Barbara was the youngest daughter of the late Johann Michael Bach, who had ended his career as organist and town clerk of Gehren near Arnstadt, and was described by Bach in his family tree, the *Genealogy*, as *an able composer*. Perhaps she was the *young woman who was a stranger to the town* whom Bach had let into the organ loft the year before to general disapproval.

The church in Dornheim near Arnstadt where Bach was married.
Charcoal drawing by Georg Renger

Bach's move to Mühlhausen, north-west of Arnstadt, to succeed Johann Georg Ahle, who was known chiefly as a vocal composer, was a step up in the world. The importance of the post, which had a long tradition behind it, is illustrated by the official commission that he immediately received for the inauguration of the new town council in February 1708. For this occasion he composed the cantata BWV 71, *Gott ist mein König* (*The Lord is my king*), which was unusually printed complete in its full score at the council's expense; this was Bach's first published work. He was asked to suggest immediate improvements for the renovation of the organ he was to play.

MARRIAGE

Report on an organ, 21 February 1708: Bach's manuscript suggestions for the renovation of the organ of the church of St Blasius in Mühlhausen. From an early age Bach was recognised as an organ expert, and he remained unchallenged in that capacity into his old age.

The organist of the free imperial city of Mühlhausen, as in other Hanseatic towns of north Germany, was in a strong position in relation to the Kantor. He could rely on the support of the 'Musical Society', a *Collegium Musicum* originally founded by the citizens, to help the Kantor in the performance of polyphonic music, although occasionally it seems to have sidelined him.

But Bach gave notice after only a year. There has been much speculation about the reasons, particularly because his request for a discharge, dated 25 June 1708 was phrased in such a decided and almost belligerent manner. *Even though I should always have liked to work towards the goal, namely, a well-regulated church music, to the glory of God and in conformance with your wishes, and would, according to my small means, have helped out as much as possible with the church music that is growing up in almost every township, and often better than the harmony that is fashioned here, and therefore have*

Hanseatic League. Organisation founded in the late medieval period by north German towns – Bremen, Hamburg, Lübeck, and others – to protect their trading instruments. The league dominated commercial activity in northern Europe from the 13th to the 15th century, with over 150 towns participating at some point.

acquired from far and wide, not without cost, a good store of the choicest church compositions, just as I have also fulfilled my duty in delivering the project for remedying the faults of the organ and should gladly have discharged every other duty of my office – yet it has not been possible to accomplish all this without hindrance, and there are, at present, hardly any signs that in the future a change may take place (although it would rejoice the souls belonging to this very Church); to which I should humbly add that, however simple my manner of living, I can live but poorly, considering the house rent and other most necessary expenses.[11] Typically, Bach makes all his points in a single sentence: not only, he says, has he done his duty as organist but this time, in contrast to his work in Arnstadt, he has paid serious attention to the performance of polyphonic music which was not even in his contract and to that end he has acquired a good stock of music. None the less, conditions were so unfavourable that the music sounded worse than village church music, rendering Bach unable to achieve his ultimate goal of providing good sacred music. The fact that his salary had also proved inadequate he deems unworthy of more than passing mention.

Bach's reasoning sounds professional enough to suggest that he was justified in looking for grounds to leave Mühlhausen. The age-old assumption was that Bach left Mühlhausen after only a year to avoid becoming embroiled in a theological controversy among the local clergy between orthodoxy and Pietism. More likely the Weimar court seemed an attractive new field of activity.

Drawing up a list of Bach's early compositions for keyboard and organ is difficult, because they have survived only in manuscript form. Very few compositions can be even approximately dated from the sources, and these are principally pieces found in two books of keyboard and organ music compiled shortly after 1700 by Bach's brother Johann Christoph for his own use, some of them written out by Johann Sebastian.[12] But in general, only the secondary sources are extant. These sources are the result of the flourishing exchange of manuscript copies between contemporary

Perhaps the earliest preserved autograph manuscript: the opening of the organ chorale *Wie schön leuchtet der Morgenstern* (*How fair the morning star doth shine*), BWV 739. The handwriting, which can be dated to between 1703 and 1705, is already extremely confident.

organists: they copied from each other, made changes, produced new versions, and certainly did not always stop to wonder whether a piece ascribed to Johann Sebastian Bach was really by him.

Despite much uncertainty, the essential facts are clear. Perhaps the most important is that Bach obviously wanted to train himself as extensively as possible in the field of organ music. Although some individual pieces were clearly written with a particular teacher in mind – Pachelbel, Georg Böhm, Johann Adam Reinken or Buxtehude – a general tendency emerges suggesting that Bach did not want to ally himself with any one school, but wished it to be clear from an early stage that he was constructing his own edifice founded on the broadest traditions. Even Bach's early work shows that he considered it outdated for a particular style of organ music to be associated with a particular landscape in the same way as reed-thatched roofs were typical of north Germany and shingle roofs of the south. In this sense, composing for the organ was no longer to be learnt as a craft: Bach saw it as a universal art, like the whole of his oeuvre, integrating the essentials of music and instrument in as concentrated a form as possible.

In his attempts at integration the young Bach was primarily concerned to unite the north and south German styles. The pre-eminence of the organist and the tonal possibilities of his instrument were typical of north Germany. Bach was clearly fascinated by the *stylus phantasticus*, which allowed the organist to be an expressive improviser or rhapsodist. (With this kind of performance, Buxtehude made his organ-playing so exciting that by the end of the 17th century he could give small secular recitals, enabling the organist to be seen as a virtuoso playing for a fee. The merchants of Lübeck would listen to him before going about their financial business in the morning.)

Bach's first organ: the double-manual instrument of the *Neukirche* in Arnstadt. It was at this organ that Bach first performed his own works.

More typically, south German and Italian features were aspects such as clear themes, transparent structure and wide-ranging harmonic disposition. Bach also drew on selected north German and Italian sources for his study of a third factor: counterpoint. He turned to strict counterpoint of sonatas by Giovanni Legrenzi, Arcangelo Corelli and Tommaso Albinoni, as well as Reinken, who had himself been influenced by these and other Italian composers.[13] It is no coincidence that double counterpoint features in his arrangements and adaptations of individual compositions; its use made a particularly economical approach to the thematic material possible.

Two organ works which are frequently played today and can be dated, reliably, to Bach's early period reflect the situation at the beginning of his career. One, the *Toccata in D minor* BWV 565, perhaps composed for harpsichord in the first place, stands principally for the expressive factor; the other, the *Prelude and Fugue in C major* BWV 531, for the principle of order. Non-specialists may find it difficult to believe that the *Toccata,* a famous work arranged for full orchestra in the 20th century by Leopold Stokowski, was composed so early. The fantastically virtuoso and sensuously tonal nature of the north German organ style is dominant, and to quote Hermann Keller, there is 'no other example of such a gripping opening as that of the *Toccata,* with its *unisono* descending like a lightning flash, the long roll of thunder of the broken chords of the full organ, and the stormy undulation of the triplets. For four bars, Bach moves furiously up and down in the diminished seventh chord, until the pedal takes over with powerful gravity.'[14] The fugue, which occupies the central part of the work, makes a less striking impression, but by linking it thematically with the opening of the *Toccata* Bach also makes his formal intentions clear.

They are even clearer in the *Prelude and Fugue in C major,* a less dazzling work but one that points to Bach's creative future. Here, perhaps for the first time, Bach dispenses with the combination of sections in the nature of free improvisation and contrapuntal sections, which was a feature of the north German organ toccata. Instead, he keeps the prelude and fugue clearly distinct, so that each can develop its own structure and character. The prelude – far removed from the *stylus phantasticus* – has the regular flow of movement so characteristic of the later Bach; the fugue, although it does have a short toccata-like conclusion, is extended and greatly developed.

Relatively speaking, a lot is known about Bach's early organ chorales from an extensive book of chorales comprising works by various composers, collected by the Thuringian organist Johann Georg Neumeister in about 1800. This contains 38 chorale arrange-

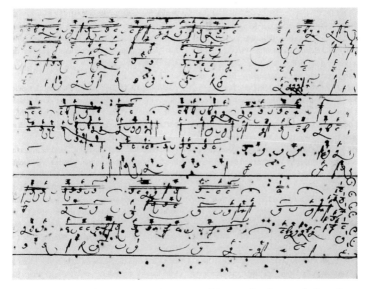

A piece of north German organ tablature: Bach's notes for the conclusion of a *Fantasia in C minor*, perhaps composed by himself (BWV Anh II, 45), in the so-called *Andreas Bach Book*. The handwriting, which can be placed at c.1706, shows Bach's familiarity with north German practice in musical notation.

ments (BWV 1090–1120) under the name of Johann Sebastian Bach; they show him well on his way to the organ chorales of his Weimar period.[15]

While, despite the problematical state of the records, a quite extensive number of Bach's early organ compositions survive, genuine early cantatas are few and far between. This is not necessarily just because of gaps in the records, but reflects the fact that as an organist the young Bach was not obliged to compose music for ordinary Sunday services. Consequently his early cantatas, with two exceptions, BWV 4 *Christ lag in Todesbanden* (*Christ lay in bonds of death*), and BWV 150 *Nach dir, Herr, verlanget mich* (*I long for thee, O Lord*), must be regarded as commissions for special occasions. Cantata BWV 196, *Der Herr denket an uns* (*The Lord is mindful of us*), might have been a wedding cantata, and BWV 106, known as the *Actus tragicus*

EARLY CANTATAS

opening with the words *Gottes Zeit ist die allerbeste Zeit* (*God's time is the best of times*), may have been written for a funeral. Cantatas BWV 71 *Gott ist mein König* (*The Lord is my king*) and BWV 131 *Aus der Tiefen rufe ich* (*Out of the depths I call unto thee*), are certainly from the Mühlhausen period: the first, as already mentioned, was composed for the inauguration of the new town council; and the second was requested by the pastor Eilmar, for some unknown occasion.

The cantatas are almost exclusively drawn from the Bible or chorales. The compositions themselves betray the influence of north and central German composers, but have their own individual stamp. Bach was already surprisingly confident in his treatment of form and could depict emotion and character with great refinement: his handling of the theme of death, in the *Actus tragicus* cantata is remarkably varied, eloquent and subtle. This setting of the words *Du wollest dem Feinde nicht geben die Seele deiner Turteltauben* (*Thou wilt not deliver up the soul of thy turtle doves to the enemy*) from the cantata written for the inauguration of the new town council is a surprising example of pictorial and sensitive lyricism, atypical of this period.

The lively Capriccio BWV 992, was composed for the departure of his beloved brother Johann Jakob, a piece of programme music, with explanatory comments on the incidents it depicts written on the manuscript: the pain of parting, fears of possible dangers, the blowing of the posthorn, and so on. The vivid tone-painting of this work, which Goethe admired, has puzzled many who failed to appreciate its humour, and maybe the mockery of its model, the *Musicalische Vorstellung einiger biblischer Historien* (*Musical presentation of certain Biblical stories*) by Johann Kuhnau, Kantor of St Thomas's, a very popular keyboard work of the time, although it was considered rather old-fashioned.

Court organist and Konzertmeister: Bach in Weimar
1708–1717

It is not known whether Bach had a formal audition before moving to Weimar in July 1708; the *Obituary* simply states that he played for the duke. In any case, he was now a court organist and chamber musician. His rise from the small town of Arnstadt to the well-salaried post in the ducal capital might well have seemed meteoric. Now he even had a recently renovated organ available in the castle church. However, Bach's place was not only in the organ gallery in the soaring vault of the *Himmelsburg* (Heaven's Castle), as the church was known because of a fresco on its ceiling showing Heaven opening up; as a court chamber musician he also had to play secular music with the ensemble. His main instrument here was the harpsichord, but he certainly would also have played the violin, viola or gamba when required.

At this time, the Weimar court Kapelle had 14 regular members. Besides the Kapellmeister, deputy Kapellmeister and concertmaster

The scene of Bach's activities in Weimar: the ducal castle, known as the *Wilhelmsburg*, before the fire of 1774. Anonymous gouache and ink drawing

there were four violinists, one bassoonist and six singers. The eight trumpeters and drummers would have been recruited part time from the military for both the church music and the chamber music.

Bach moved into the house of fellow musician Adam Immanuel Weldig on the Marktplatz; there, he led the life of a solid middle-class paterfamilias. His daughter Catharina Dorothea was born at the end of 1708, and his eldest son Wilhelm Friedemann two years later. In 1713, Maria Barbara had twins, who died tragically early. Bach's sons Carl Philipp Emanuel and Johann Gottfried Bernhard were born in the springs of 1714 and 1715 respectively. Godfather to the elder of the two boys was Georg Philipp Telemann, the composer with whom, according to his godson's later reminiscences, Bach 'often kept company in his youth'. In 1738 Bach described Johann Gottfried as a son who was *alas! Misguided*. At that time the young man had compounded his other offences by leaving his position as organist in Sangerhausen without notice, and he died the next year of a 'hot fever'.[16]

The court musician Adam Immanuel Weldig was a male soprano. When they could not afford *castrati*, rulers often employed male sopranos, who were also sought-after members of urban choirs. During his time in Leipzig, Bach worked with male sopranos including Christian Friedrich Schemelli.

In Weimar, Bach found god-parents for his children, became the godfather to other people's children himself, and made friends with citizens of Weimar including Johann Gottfried Walther, the city organist, art connoisseur and, later, lexicographer. He examined organs, taught and travelled to performances of music at the nearby court of Weissenfels. However, after only a

Johann Gottfried Walther (1684–1748), a distant relative of Bach, worked as a municipal organist and royal tutor in Weimar. He shared Bach's interests in musical theory, the art of the strict score and the vocal polyphony of Palestrina. The National Library of Berlin holds a manuscript of Palestrina's *Missa Ecce sacerdos*, which Walther and Bach allegedly worked on together. Bach later included this manuscript in his music library.

few years he felt the urge to leave Weimar. At the end of 1713, he successfully applied for the prestigious post of organist at the Church of Our Lady, in Halle.

Ultimately he turned the post down, unable to negotiate a satisfactory salary. However, if anything this application seems to have enhanced his standing at the Weimar court. A post of *Konzertmeister* was created for him, and, thus, he he was promoted from one of the lowest positions in the Kapelle hierarchy to the third highest. The appointment, made in March 1714, brought a considerable pay rise, and required him to compose a church cantata every month and to rehearse it with the Kapelle. This task had traditionally been the duty of the deputy Kapellmeister; perhaps he had not carried it out satisfactorily, or perhaps the idea was merely to provide him with competition.

The church authorities in Halle were disappointed by Bach's refusal of the post, and accused him of mere tactical manoeuvring; in a letter of 19 March 1714 he denied this vigorously. The conditions prevailing at the court in Weimar were difficult, so it was not impossible that Bach would have been happy to go to Halle but was forced by the reigning Duke Wilhelm Ernst to stay and keep quiet about his situation. The duke was not sole ruler of the duchy but had to share sovereignty with his nephew Ernst August, son of Johann Ernst. Even the court musicians became involved in the turmoil of a bitter power struggle between uncle and nephew: the elder duke forbade them to work for the younger, while the younger – who was particularly fond of music – threatened reprisals if they obeyed his uncle's orders. An extreme case involved the horn player Adam Andreas Reichhardt: when he tried to give notice he was condemned to a hundred lashes and imprisoned, and after he had finally left the court – in secret – he was declared an outlaw and hanged in effigy.[17]

Against this grim background, it is not surprising that in the autumn of 1717, when Bach himself asked to leave the ducal service, he was imprisoned for nearly a month and dishonourably discharged. According to the Weimar court records: 'On November 6, the quondam *Konzertmeister* and organist Bach was confined to the County Judge's place of detention for too stubbornly forcing the issue of his dismissal and, finally, on December 2 was freed from arrest with notice of his unfavourable discharge.'[18]

The last straw may have been the death of the Kapellmeister Johann Samuel Drese at the end of 1716 – Duke Wilhelm Ernst obviously intended Drese's son and deputy to succeed him. Even if Wilhelm Ernst was merely conforming with a principle of tenure, Bach must have seen it as a slight. Furthermore, Duke Ernst August may have been interested in the very popular Georg Philipp Telemann for the post, as Telemann himself mentions in general terms in Johann Mattheson's *Ehrenpforte* of 1740.

When Bach later deplored the fact that the *authorities are odd* in Leipzig, he may have felt that he had already experienced similar oddity in Weimar – perhaps even in Arnstadt and Mühlhausen. It was certainly no coincidence that at the beginning of Cantata No 84, *Ich bin vergnügt mit meinem Glücke, das mir der liebe Gott beschert* (*I am content with the fortune that the good Lord gives me*), written in Leipzig, he changed the original wording of his librettist Picander, who had written, 'Ich bin vergnügt mit meinem Stande, den mir der liebe Gott beschert'. ('I am content with the profession the Lord has given me'). Bach must have had to seek his fortune elsewhere, perhaps in his creative work. The question is how did all of the composer's professional problems – whether imposed upon him or of his own making – affect his creative work?

Picander is one of the few Bach librettists known by name today. The librettist of the Leipzig cantatas has not been positively identified: some of the first year's texts were probably composed by the former mayor Gottfried Lange, and the second year's perhaps by Andreas Stübel, ex-deputy head teacher at the *Thomasschule*. Bach only used printed libretto collections in exceptional cases.

In point of fact, hardly any of the great composers can be said to have led a 'happy life'. Admittedly, some German composers organised the course of their lives very efficiently, among them Georg Philipp Telemann, Carl Philipp Emanuel Bach and Joseph Haydn; some, like Mozart, were adept at seizing the pleasure of the moment. But in general the image of creative artists is one of people at odds with themselves and the world. The words of Beethoven, written on the title page of his piano and cello sonata Op 69 – 'Inter lacrimas et luctum' ('Between tears and mourning') – or Wagner's 'In Noth und Sorgen' ('In distress and sorrow') at the end of his draft of *The Flying Dutchman*, reflect the rule rather than the exception.

There is much to suggest that the melancholy and vulnerability of many great German musicians after Bach stimulated their creative imaginations. Such composers also performed a covert social function: complaining about the burden of life was taboo, regarded as aberrant in a milieu fuelled by the optimism of progressive ideas. Such complaints could best be expressed in the comforting medium of music, particularly sacred works in which Christian lamentations on the misery of earthly life *sub specie aeternitatis* had always been legitimate.

These ideas lead back to Bach himself. If his life had run a more regular course, perhaps he would have written as many compositions as Telemann. Perhaps he would not have tired so quickly when trying to complete major projects – for instance, in his work on the *Orgelbüchlein* (*Little Organ Book*) and the first cycle of cantatas during his Weimar period. Perhaps in later years, he would not have resorted so much to parody works – that is, making 'new' compositions of old ones by re-using the old music with new texts. Perhaps he would even have written an opera. Perhaps he would have made sure that more good editions of his works were printed during his lifetime – so that Bach studies need not have concentrated so much on research into the sources, as they must to this day.

However, would we have been any better off for having a Bach of that nature – quite apart from the fact that by now we can hardly imagine such a composer? He had his difficulties and took them hard, he was upset by them and then worked through them. We can tell as much from his music: it is not music that was written lightly, but allows us to guess at the effort it took the composer to 'let go' in a kind of adagio remote from all earthly concerns. Bach shows a humanity in that dimension which is very similar to Beethoven's. Would history have thought better of a completed *Die Kunst der Fuge* (*The Art of Fugue*) rather than the fragmentary work that was Bach's last attempt to explore the profundities of music in terms of number and feeling, sense and sensuality?

The greater part of Bach's oeuvre has come down in undated manuscripts, so compiling a catalogue of the Weimar compositions presents much the same problem that arises in the cataloguing and assessment of his early work. However, we are better informed about the details because more works are involved. We can approximate Bach's achievements in the years when he was first producing masterpieces, although many questions must remain, particularly in his music for instrumental ensembles.

As court organist he continued the compositional activities on which he had embarked in Arnstadt, writing organ pieces. But now, and for the first time, the systematic approach so characteristic of the later Bach became evident. Increasingly, he liked to think and write in series and cycles. About 1710, he began a volume of organ chorales (BWV 599–644), though not adding a title page until he had moved to Köthen:

> *Little Organ Book*
> *In which a Beginner at the organ is given*
> *Instruction in Developing a Chorale*
> *in many diverse ways, and at the same time*
> *in Acquiring Facility in the Study of the Pedal*

since in the Chorales contained therein
the Pedal is treated as Wholly Obbligato.
In Praise of the Almighty's Will
And for my Neighbour's Greater Skill

Autore Joanne Sebast. Bach
p.t. [pleno titulo] Capellae Magistri
Serenissimi Principis Regnantis
Anhaltini-Cotheniensis.[19]

On the empty pages of the volume, Bach wrote the opening words of 164 chorales arranged according to the church year. However, over the years, only about a quarter of these titles was completed, the last of them probably written in his Leipzig period. This was characteristic of Bach: to begin great undertakings and to tire of them before they were completed. Admittedly, in this case the reason may be that after finishing 46 pieces he had said everything he had to say.

Albert Schweitzer describes the *Orgelbüchlein* as 'one of the greatest events in all music'. No composer before Bach, who was then barely 30 years old, and hardly any after him worked on so many different levels. First, he successfully merged the style of the north German organ chorale, which imitated the articulation of the solo vocal music with the central German chorale fuguette, thus integrating two major strands of his contemporaneous musical tradition. Second, he took the familiar text of whatever hymn concerned him as a point of departure for musical settings rich in emotion, style and sensuous tone-painting. Schweitzer noted of the *Orgelbüchlein* it is 'the dictionary of Bach's musical language'.[20] Third, he gave each of the organ chorales such an individual and

The figurative nature of the *Orgelbüchlein* chorales surfaces throughout the pieces. In the Christmas song 'This joyful day' the middle voices seem to imitate a hand rocking the infant Christ's cradle. In the chorale *Through Adam's fall it's corrupted* original sin is illustrated by an almost unbearably hard harmony.

unmistakable character that the *Orgelbüchlein* may be seen as anticipating the music of the 19th century, even the late bagatelles of Beethoven. The character pieces or songs without words of other composers seem rather one-dimensional in the face of such a wealth of inspiration.

As well as the *Orgelbüchlein*, Bach composed a series of other arrangements of hymns for organ in Weimar, many of them on a larger scale. Later he revised some of these works in Leipzig in a manuscript known as the 'Eighteen Chorales', BWV 651–668, although strictly speaking he completed only 17 arrangements. Naturally, he wrote original organ works in Weimar,[21] including BWV 532, 534–538, 540–545, 548–550 and 564, (most of his major works in that genre). In addition, in 1713–14 he made five organ and sixteen harpsichord arrangements of instrumental concerti by other composers such as Antonio Vivaldi, Giuseppe Torelli, Benedetto Marcello, Telemann and Prince Johann Ernst of Weimar (BWV 592–596, 972–987).[22] These provide an invaluable window into German ornamentation of concertante music at the time, particularly Bach's inspired elaboration of Marcello's D minor oboe concerto.

The Bolognese violinist Guiseppe Torelli (1658–1709) served as *Konzertmeister* to the Margrave of Brandenburg from 1698–9. His *Concerti Musicali Op 66* were the first true violin concerti; his preface to the pieces marks the birth of the orchestral concertante style: 'Note that wherever you find the word *Solo* in the concerto, you must play it with one violin alone. For the rest, the parts may be doubled, or even re-enforced by three or four instruments apiece.'

In 1714, Bach's organ was restored by the organ builder Nikolaus Trebs, this time to his own liking. The specification can be approximated.[23] With its two manuals, the instrument at which Bach spent the crucial years of his career as an organist was not exactly a large organ suitable for virtuoso performance in the north German tradition, but one that may have corresponded to his liking for polyphonic setting:

Oberwerk C-c³	Brustwerk C-c³	Pedal C-d¹
Quintadena 16'	Prinzipal 8'	Grossuntersatz 32'
Prinzipal 8'	Viola da gamba 8'	Subbass 16'
Gemshorn 8'	Gedackt 8'	Violonbass 16'
Gedackt 8'	Kleingedackt 4'	Prinzipal 8'
Quintadena 4'	Oktave 4'	Cornettbass 4'
Oktave 4'	Waldflöte 2'	Posaune 16'
Mixtur × 6	Sesquialtera × 4	Trompete 8'
Zimbel 3fach	Trompete 8'	Glockenspiel

Zimbelstern
Tremulant in both manuals

The list of vocal compositions that Bach wrote in his early Weimar years is incomplete. Probably the earliest of the extant cantatas is a genre piece, the *Jagdkantate* (*Hunt Cantata*) BWV 208. Bach composed it in or after 1712 for the birthday of Duke Christian of Saxe-Weissenfels, at whose court it was first performed by Bach himself. This secular work, written very much in courtly style, approaches the modern Italian-style formal scheme of vocal music determined by recitative and the *da capo* aria. Both in tone and in the orchestral musical forces he employed, his musical language is careful to provide an elegant entertainment suitable for performance at court.[24]

When he was made *Konzertmeister*, Bach faced the appointed task of composing and performing a church cantata every month.[25] He set to work with a will, exactly as he had with the *Orgelbüchlein*, as if he had just been waiting to show his ability not only as organist but also as the composer of sacred pieces for holy days. Most of the texts were provided by

The famous *Hunt cantata* aria, dedicated to the Duke Christian of Saxe-Weissenfels, sounds very idyllic:

Sheep can safely graze
where a gentle shepherd keeps watch.
Where rulers rule well,
Subjects feel peace and quiet,
And countries are happy.

Unfortunately, the duke praised in this song brought such economic ruin on his lands that a royal commission had to take charge of his financial administration.

In Bach's day, Pietism was extremely popular among the Protestant nobility. Philipp Jacob Spender, father of German Pietism and for some time the court chaplain of Dresden, consulted many aristocrats about religious matters. Back then, Pietism denoted not a sect, but a movement in Lutheran churches.

Salomon Franck, court poet and consistorial secretary of Weimar, who had a good reputation as the author of hymns, libretti and cantatas. In contrast to Erdmann Neumeister, the leading cantata librettist of the time, Franck's religious faith was expressed continually and he had a particularly mystical devotion to the person of Christ. Bach, who was no more a Pietist than Franck, may well have found his approach inspiring, even if not identifying with Franck's highly-charged writing. However, figurative language full of feeling offered more inspiration to a composer than the dry paraphrases of Biblical texts.

From the first work of this series, the cantata BWV 182, *Himmelskönig, sei willkommen* (*Welcome, King of Heaven*), written for Palm Sunday 1714, Bach shows an expressive variety of form. The magnificent orchestral introduction, an echo of French 'overtures', employs the courtly style appropriate to divine service at the court of Weimar. The chorus that follows observes the form of the modern Italian *da capo* aria without abandoning the traditional fugal element.

The three arias with obbligato accompaniments that follow are examples of both vocal virtuosity and exquisite chamber music textures; the first two have the character of dances, whilst the passionate third raises the edifying Pietistic hymn to operatic heights. In contrast, the effect of the subsequent chorale arrangement, *Jesu, deine Passion* (*Jesus, thy Passion*), is as if a piece from the *Orgelbüchlein* had been transformed into a chorale movement in the nature of a motet, while the final dance-like *So lasset uns gehen in Salem der Freuden* (*So let us enter the Salem of gladness*), again in *da capo* form, takes on the function of a cheerful closing dance, even though the framework of the movement is fugal.

Other works written in 1714 show a similar richness of form and expression. They include BWV 12, *Weinen, Klagen, Sorgen, Zagen* (*Weeping, wailing, sorrowing, hesitating*), with its chromatic *lamento* bass, and BWV 61, *Nun komm, der Heiden Heiland* (*Come, Saviour of the heathen*), where the French overture form is directly applied to a chorale movement for chorus. Perhaps Bach's aim was to unite the old and the new, courtly magnificence and solid craftsmanship, the grand and the intimate, operatic and sacred styles, showing the composer as an artist drawing inspiration from tradition but still keeping up with the times, a man able to speak the language of music profoundly in a manner all his own.

Because Bach's Weimar cantatas rank among the finest that he ever composed, it is not surprising that he performed them in Leipzig again. Under pressure to play a different cantata every Sunday, Bach also occasionally fell back on his Weimar pieces out of sheer relief.

Bach, who had to compose and perform one cantata every four weeks, tried to arrange his delivery dates so that in time he would assemble a complete series of cantatas for all the Sundays and holy days of the church year, and initially he worked consistently with this idea in mind.

Today the names of some 20 cantatas for an annual cycle written in Weimar are known. Some separate occasional compositions have clearly been lost, as well as a Passion (BC D 1), probably written for Gotha, parts of which Bach apparently re-used for the *St John Passion*.

We can only speculate about what instrumental music Bach composed in Weimar. A copy in his hand of a two-violin concerto by Telemann has been preserved. Bach probably gave it to the violinist Johann Georg Pisendel as a present when Pisendel visited him in Weimar in 1709.[26] We may deduce from this that he must have been

Controversy has arisen recently about the existence of a contemporaneous *Passion* for Gotha. Some scholars doubt that Bach incorporated arias from the *Gothaer Passion* into the second version of the *St John Passion* of 1725, claiming that Bach composed these arias for the first time in Leipzig. It is clear, in any event, that the central *Mensch, wein für Deine Sünden* does not derive from the *Gothaer Passion*, for Bach in his Weimar period had not yet experimented much with complicated vocal settings.

Bach's place of work as court organist and *Konzertmeister*: the interior of the Weimar castle church, with the organ in the top gallery. Gouache by Christian Richter, *c.*1660

interested in that genre. Perhaps he was writing such compositions himself. Maybe Bach approached the concerto genre hesitantly at first, working out its stylistic principle in keyboard and organ music, including the arrangements of instrumental concerti. After all, he did not present himself as a composer of concerti, sonatas and suites until he moved to Köthen.

EXCURSUS: BACH'S MUSICAL STYLE

In contrast to the partially preserved early work, the extant oeuvre from Bach's Weimar period is extensive, and well defined enough to clarify his personal constants. Essential basic concepts are those of all-*in*-one and all-*from*-one. The former is evident in Bach's tendency to combine heterogeneous genres in a single work, the latter in his compulsion to draw maximum musical substance from as little material as possible. The closing movement of cantata BWV 182, *So lasset uns gehen in Salem der Freuden*, which is fairly bland in character, may serve as an example of the first concept. By nature, it is a *gigue* in the construction of a fugue with strict permutations; its total structure is of a concerto movement, divided into *tutti* and solo sections, the overall form in turn being determined by the A-B-A scheme of the *da capo* aria. Extreme examples of the all-from-one concept are Bach's riddle or enigmatic canons, one of which, BWV 1073, is from the Weimar period. Here, a few notes suffice to provide the code for an entire, if short, composition.

Four main principles to which Bach characteristically felt bound can be distinguished within his general idea: the concertante principle; the obbligato principle; the rhetorical principle; and the symbolical principle. All four can be traced back to the musical theory and practice of Bach's time, but in their mutual interplay and the forcefulness of their presentation are typical only of Bach himself.

The concertante principle dominated much music of the Baroque era. It originated in Italian music of the late-16th and early-17th centuries, particularly Venetian polychoral practice. Earlier, the principle of polyphonic setting expressed in the motet genre had been dominant. It has been compared to a fabric in which the separate parts are threads of equal importance, whereas now the tapestry – to continue the same image – was no longer woven as a single whole but assembled from brightly coloured pieces. The process did not produce a random patchwork but a simple, well-proportioned pattern similar to the patterns of folk music – for an important aspect of the new style was that art music should be tuneful and as easily understood as folk music.

Giovanni Gabrieli developed Venetian polychorality in his church music, a technique adopted by Heinrich Schütz in his large double-chorus pieces – for example, his late *Magnificat* – and by Johann Sebastian Bach in his late motets – notably, *Singet dem Herrn ein neues Lied*. In the 19th century, Johannes Brahms took up this style in his *Fest- und Gedenksprüche*.

Folk music employs the alternation of high and low voices, different groups, chorus and soloist, or soloists alternating with each other. Early concerted music uses much the same methods, with different choirs and groups of voices alternating and then coming together again – an effect visually expressed in Venice, where the musicians could be placed in the various choirs of St Mark's. 'Colour' came from the wide-ranging harmonies that fitted the parts into clearly distinct, homophonic blocks; if a composer made use of the different registers of the human voice, or added the variegated sounds of different instruments, he had further possibilities to make a structure from musical colour.

In the instrumental music, which gradually came to the fore in adopting the concertante principle, a tendency towards succinctness became evident in the course of the 17th century. As a result, not long after 1700, the Italian solo concerto 'in the Vivaldi style' emerged from the plethora of concerto forms that had been tried out in practice. Just as the unchanging refrain of a folk-song alternates with the verses, which are different each time, the orchestral ritornello alternated with the various solo episodes in a concerto. The ritornello – literally, 'little return' – gradually acquired a standard

tripartite form: the opening, the continuation and the cadence. Although Vivaldi and his Italian contemporaries differentiated and experimented with the sequence of keys and with motifs within this scheme, they understood concerto form as basically functional. In that capacity, the concerto provided both orchestra and a number of soloists a chance to present themselves in as striking a way as possible.

The Italian concerto swiftly conquered Europe, particularly the

The great pioneer of the concerto: Antonio Vivaldi. Pen and ink drawing by Leone Ghezzi, 1723 princely courts where the elite ensembles were better suited to the performance of this new music than were town musicians or the *Collegia Musica* of the middle classes. Bach had the opportunity to study and practise it in Weimar if not before, since the duke was extremely keen on Italian concerti. Some years before Bach's arrival as court organist and harpsichordist, the duke had sent his future deputy Kapellmeister, Johann Wilhelm Drese, to study in Venice for eight months and bring back sheet music. Clear evidence of Bach's interest in the Italian solo concerto is provided by his arrangements for organ and harpsichord, which he made probably not only for study purposes but at the request of young Prince Johann Ernst of Weimar (who died soon afterwards), who liked to hear instrumental concerti, transcribed for a keyboard instrument.

Clearly Bach was not concerned merely with mastering the functions of the concerto and composing examples himself. He was fascinated by concertante form itself, and finding ways of making it a constructional principle in his own works. This question obsessed Bach all his life: how could he work with the concertante principle, how could he use it to create concise but subtly differentiated forms suitable for representing processes of musical development? He was not concerned with enabling music, rendered functional by the presence of text, song tunes and choreography, to attain structural 'autonomy', but rather with clearly determining the nature of that autonomous factor in the context of modern music. The point under discussion was not fixed form – making its own laws, for instance, the traditional fugue – but the use of forms that took as their material the opposition between the static and the dynamic, the permanent and the transitory, the constant and the variable, objective factors and subjective factors arising from the freedom of the chosen subject.

The perfectly proportioned structure of the C-major fugue from the *Well-Tempered Clavier* has been related to the philosophical views of Gottfried Wilhelm Leibniz and his ideas of 'pre-stabilised harmony'.[27] But our concern is less with the universalism, owing allegiance to medieval traditions that would influence Bach's thinking and writing in later years, than with strategies of composition at the time of the Enlightenment. Man was arduously assessing and reshaping his opportunities in the form of his own ideas, in his own image. Bach was anticipating concepts that, two generations later, would make sonata form the focal point of the musical thinking of the 'great' German composers.

Obviously Bach did not primarily develop the concertante principle in instrumental ensemble music, but initially within his own genre of keyboard music. As we can see from, for instance, the *Dorian Toccata* BWV 538, or the *Toccata in C major* BWV 564, the original organ works of the Weimar period were clearly influenced by the outline of the concerto. The second of these works was already a fully-fledged 'concerto' in several movements, with its sequence of toccata, adagio and fugue. Not only does the opening movement follow the concerto scheme, the final movement too can be described as a 'concertante fugue'.[28]

Gottfried Willhelm Leibniz (1646–1716) was a mathematician and philosopher who developed a theory of calculus concomitant with – but independent of – Newton's. In metaphysical works such as *The Monadology* (1714), he argued that everything in the universe was comprised of innumerable units, or *monads*, that determined the objects' past, present and future.

Bach proceeds in much the same way in his organ music when it is based on cantus firmus. In the organ chorale *Nun komm, der Heiden Heiland*, BWV 660a, the hymn tune is built into a movement that derives its structure from a ritornello that divides it up and is obtained itself from that cantus firmus.[29] Bach was much concerned with the concertante principle in his Weimar cantatas as well, of course, as in his later work. For instance, this is evident, in most of the movements of cantata BWV 182, mentioned above, *Himmelskönig, sei willkommen*, whether they are purely instrumental, choral or solo numbers.

One does not usually speak of the principle of obbligato writing until the time of Viennese classicism. Heinrich Christoph Koch, in a manual on composition published in 1792, praises Mozart's 1785 string quartets as the quintessence of the genre, since they 'are handled in the manner of a fugue' and 'really consist of four obbligato parts, none of which quarrels with the others for pre-eminence as the main voice'.[30] The background to his comment was a definition of the entire Baroque period as the 'age of the *basso continuo*' that was still influential in Mozart's time. This doctrine held that the composition proceeds from a harmonic 'foundation', the *basso continuo* that runs regularly through it, with one or more melodic parts rising above it. In short, musical composition of the Baroque age tended to be reduced to a framework of 'melody' and harmonic 'accompaniment'.

Bach also took *basso continuo* for granted, as the basis of contemporary composition, and taught it in that sense, as we can see from the rules for the *basso* technique copied out by his wife Anna Magdalena and his son Johann Christoph in their appendix to the *Klavierbüchlein* he compiled. At the same time, however, he appropriated the inheritance of pre-Baroque music, which understood musical setting as the working together and against each other of equal voices. These voices require no particular harmonic foundation

Since approximately 1600, the Italian term *basso continuo* has been used to describe the harmonic behaviour of the instrumental bass voice in a composition. One of Bach's pupils, Johann Peter Keller, preserved a manuscript entitled 'Regulations and Principles for the four-part playing of the thorough bass.'

because they come together, as if of themselves, as a result of the part-writing. It is in this sense that Bach himself speaks of the obbligato *parts* of the three-part *Inventions*. Except in a fugue, obbligato setting is not particularly concerned with developing all the parts out of a single theme, but in general with handling them independently, and also independently of any harmonic bass-line running with them.

OBBLIGATO SETTING

The whole idea basically expresses an aesthetic, if not a philosophical problem. Unusually for his time, Bach takes it as a theme and pits himself against the Enlightenment, which advocated the natural and the comprehensible in music, as in all other fields. Yet what could be more natural and comprehensible than a melody above a choral accompaniment? On the other hand, a structure consisting of three or more equal parts, whilst expressing a more confident and logical way of dealing with musical material, makes more demands on the audience. In Bach's Leipzig period a controversy (to which we shall come later) flared up on the question of whether the famous master was not going too far in making good music difficult.

To Bach, obbligato setting meant basically writing in three parts. Even at an early stage he was interested in the trio sonatas of north German and Italian origin. In Weimar, even in Leipzig he continued to arrange instrumental trio sonatas for the organ. In addition, he composed trios for organ in order to demonstrate the validity of the motto 'Three keyboards, three parts' by three-part performance on an organ with two manuals and pedal. This kind of composition still struck him as so important that in his early Leipzig period he composed the six organ sonatas BWV 525–590, according to tradition, as a kind of artistic dowry for his son Wilhelm Friedemann, and in the last years of his life he published the works known as the *Schübler Chorales* BWV 645–650, drawn from older cantata movements.

Naturally, three-part settings can also be found in the sonatas for melody instruments and even the concerti. In any case, such structures are essential for the type of aria with obbligato instrumental accompaniment which dominates Bach's vocal works. However, when Bach moved away from what he saw as an imbalance in the compulsory combination of *basso continuo* and melodic part, it was not merely in the direction of obbligato polyphonic writing. He felt it important to show how a melodic instrument on its own could achieve perfection by assuming both melodic and harmonic functions. The works completed in Köthen are good examples, the sonatas and partitas for solo violin BWV 1001–1006, and the suites for solo cello BWV 1007–1012.

'In general it seems as if, at this time, Bach wished to try everything that could be done with many voices and with few,' wrote his biographer Johann Nikolaus Forkel at the beginning of the 19th century.[31] A century later, Anton Webern added: 'For everything is there in Bach: the development of cyclical forms, the conquest of the realm of sound – a striving for the utmost integration.'[32] With such an attitude, Bach had bound himself to a difficult task that would take him all his life. Merely the integration of the concertante principle with the obbligato principle and its special case, the fugue, would have been such a task. Bach was always in search of new and interesting ways to give structure to his music. It is as if he actively sought out problems just in order to work through them, thus demonstrating the demands made on the human mind if it is to write polyphonic music of the highest order. At the same time, such music can be perceived in its social context and in a functional aspect as an organ chorale, concerto, cantata or aria.

It was almost perverse for a composer of the Baroque age to concern himself with problems of composition in an abstract, non-functional manner. After all, vocal genres in which the suitable rendering of a text were taken for granted were dominant at the time. But the typical composer of instrumental genres such as the concerto was chiefly concerned with the question of how, with simple but effective compositions, he might find a public ready to regard instrumental music as a pleasure in itself – and to pay accordingly. Only counterpoint of the highest nature had the luxury of non-functionality about it, but since working on such counterpoint was the privilege of a few knowledgeable experts it was expressed mainly in the making of 'books of the musical art' or the writing of difficult 'riddle' canons. But we would be seeing Bach in the wrong light if we regarded him only as the pioneer of autonomous, self-referential music, interesting though such an analysis may be.[33]

In fact Bach can also be approached from the angle of the Baroque *ars inveniendi*, the art of invention, through ideas that lie outside music, that are only partially musical or trans-musical. His music is not just structure but also speaks eloquently to the listener. The rhetorical principle that he adopted manifests itself in various dimensions, and as the confrontation of old and new traditions: the tradition of the *musica poetica*, or musical rhetoric, derived from humanism, which in its turn borrowed ideas from classical antiquity. It shows that skilfully written music can be eloquent in itself: just as a speech is adorned, its effect heightened by rhetorical figures, a composition too gains by the use of figures.

Musical rhetoric operates directly, in the tradition of Marcus Fabius Quintilianus (Quintilian) above all, with the rules of vocal rhetoric, by transferring certain sentence structures, verbal usages and so on, to musical composition. A good example is the *climax*, the heightened repetition of a musical phrase. A circular melodic movement is the *circulatio*, particularly suitable for the setting of textual passages that speak of surrounding or encircling some-

In 1979, the American researchers Ursula and Warren Kirkendale argued that in his creation of *Musical Victims* Bach used the same arrangement as the ancient rhetorician Quintilian (*c*.35–*c*.96) in his eloquent speech. Even though Bach knew Quintilian's writings from his school days it is doubtful if he really used his knowledge in this manner.

thing, of the earth or a crown. Chromatically descending sequences of fourths are known as the *passus duriusculus* ('hard passage'), indicating that it is suitable for the setting of sorrowful words. Since there was a wealth of different manuals of musical rhetoric, none of this was either obligatory or part of a self-contained system. In so far as composers used *musica poetica* at all, they did not work it out from a table of rhetorical figures, but drew freely (perhaps unconsciously) on stock figures acquired from oral tradition.

All the same, we should not underestimate the productive erudition of a few outstanding musicians, in particular Heinrich Schütz and Johann Sebastian Bach. The humanist tradition of musical rhetoric was falling into oblivion during Bach's generation, or at least was no longer regarded as practicable. What use, Enlightenment composers such as Johann Mattheson asked, was an ingeniously artificial musical work employing figures that could be seen in the notes on the page, but not heard by non-professionals as it was performed? Music was 'tonal eloquence', setting a text as naturally and intelligibly as possible, and that was to be achieved mainly by following the rhythm of language itself, the emotional content of the words, and the general style of speech. The highly educated Mattheson, who was well acquainted with the tenets of musical rhetoric, allowed it only where it enhanced the real potential of music: to move natural emotions and speak more to the senses than to the mind. He would certainly have agreed with the philosopher John Locke, who said that nothing in the reasoning mind had not been sensed previously.

We know that Bach valued, studied and sometimes performed the music of Palestrina (c.1525–94). What he knew of Heinrich Schütz (1585–1672) is unknown. The 'rhetorical' style of the *Kleine geistliche Konzerte* (*Little Sacred Concerti*) and the *sinfoniae sacrae*, which we still admire in Schütz, is to be found only in some of his ariosi. The flourishing contrapuntal style of the *Geistliche Chormusik*, however, is widely found in Bach's own choral polyphony, and the brilliant use of polychorality in Schütz's late *Magnificat* has its echo in Bach's motets for double chorus.

Bach could also, of course, write flowing melodies and emotional music in a direct and tuneful style. Such features are so evident, particularly in his Weimar period, that at this phase of Bach's career Heinrich Besseler can speak of a cantabile and expressive tonal language full of feeling, in which he anticipates *Empfindsamkeit* (the aesthetic of sensibility) and *Sturm und Drang*.[34] But for all that, he was not abandoning the *musica poetica* tradition; instead of merely satisfying the heart and the feelings, it gave musical performance a deeper sense enduring beyond the fleeting moment.

The rhetorical principle can be illustrated from almost any of Bach's works, whether vocal or instrumental. In the Weimar cantata BWV 12, *Weinen, Klagen, Sorgen, Zagen*, the introductory *Sinfonia* could be the slow movement of Vivaldian solo concerto, the 'song' of the solo oboe performing an emotional lament above the heavy fabric of sound provided by the *basso continuo* and violas, shaded by the sighing movements of the violins. This is a very modern eloquence, appealing to the mind and the senses. Admittedly Bach then resorts to the older tradition of the *musica poetica*, for in the following first chorus the model of classical rhetoric is perceptible purely from the text: the words *Weeping, wailing, sorrowing, hesitating* add up to what was known in the rhetoric of classical antiquity as an *asyndeton*, a series of associated concepts not linked by conjunctions.[35] Bach enhances the effect by having each word of the opening phrase sung by a different voice, unusually for the beginning of a choral movement. To represent the pain, he makes use among other effects of the figure of the *passus duriusculus* repeated ostinato. We can tell, from the fact that he used the same composition again in the last years of his life to set the words of the 'Crucifixus' in the *B-minor Mass*, that he was concerned to depict not only the sensuous experience but the spiritual essence behind it.

The symbolical principle can be illustrated from cantata BWV 12. In bars 85–8 in the central section of the opening chorus, the words *die das Zeichen Jesu tragen* (*those who bear the sign of Jesus*) show a striking use of the *basso continuo*: the sequence $f \mid b \mid e$ -*flat* $\mid$ a -*flat* occurs in long note values. If the note-heads of the two outer and two inner notes on the staff are linked, an X-shaped figure appears, which stands first for the cross that Christians must bear (Bach chose to write the term *Xisten* on the score of this movement), and second for *chi*, the 22nd letter of the Greek alphabet and the initial of 'Christus', much used in the chi-ro of Christian symbolism.[36]

In this case, the porous border between the rhetorical and symbolical principles in music can be made out easily. If we take the *chiastic* (crosswise) course of the basso continuo as an emblem of the true cross – on the same model as the 'Crucify' choruses in Bach's *Passions* – then one might call it a figure of musical rhetoric, the tonal sequence imitating the semantic content of a word, so to speak. If we take the 'X' as an emblem of Christ, then the direction of ideas and the viewpoint are reversed. Instead of simply copying something, the music is itself a copy, or rather a symbol. With this second aspect we are concerned with classical ideas as interpreted in a Christian sense in the Middle Ages and then passed on in Lutheran and Baroque mysticism: in this system of thought, fundamental truths are present in the symbols linked to them. In calling on the emblem, you call on what it represents. Christ appears in the letter 'X'. If this 'X' takes shape through musical notation, the idea is not to adorn the music with an artificial figure, but to show that among the functions and tasks of music is its ability to realise crucial elements of the Christian faith. In this sense, music need not actually present symbols; instead, it is itself a symbol of divine order. This idea can be deduced from the numerical relationships inherent in it, and it is one that Bach, to whatever extent, illustrates in his work.

Bach dynamically combines or forcibly integrates such heterogeneous principles as the four described above in his work, shaping it into an oeuvre that despite its vigorous interaction with concrete phenomena of intellectual, social and stylistic history has always been regarded as a unique case of music that transcends its history. Even a composer as well aware of teleological history as Wagner emphasised such features, using the *Well-Tempered Clavier* as his main example. 'Elemental forces like planets are given psychic life there; he is the musician *kat exochen* . . . Everything is contained here in the kernel . . . Bach wrote much down unconsciously, as if in a dream; the unending melody seems to have been predestined.'[37]

Court Kapellmeister in Köthen
1717–1723

In Köthen, Bach was immediately given what he had been denied in Weimar: the title of Kapellmeister and Director of Chamber Music, and, thus, control of all the music at court. His appointment was announced on 5 August 1717 but he did not actually take up the post until December, after he had been released from imprisonment in Weimar. None the less, that Bach was receiving his basic salary from August onwards may be seen as evidence of the high esteem he enjoyed at the Köthen court. The connection may have come about through Ernst August, co-regent of Weimar, who was married to a sister of Prince Leopold of Anhalt-Köthen: an art-lover, Ernst August may well have been pleased to recommend for the Köthen post a musician whose talents he certainly appreciated better than his detested uncle did.

Although Bach's life would not be free of conflict in Köthen,

his new working conditions would be the easiest he ever enjoyed in his life. Prince Leopold of Anhalt-Köthen, who was only 23 at the time and a bachelor, valued and respected Bach as a man and an artist. As early as November 1718 he, his brother and sister stood godparents to Bach's baby son Leopold August, who died in infancy. To Leopold's credit, Bach,

The grand setting for the works of Court Kapellmeister Bach: the castle of Köthen, in an engraving from Matthäus Merian's Topographia of 1650 usually so critical of authority, wrote in 1730 that when he was in Köthen he had *had a gracious Prince who both loved and knew music*. Even when Bach resigned as Kapellmeister in 1723, the parting was an amicable one; he was released from his post with all respectful ceremony and remained 'honorary Kapellmeister'. In later years, he travelled from Leipzig to Köthen on a number of occasions to perform his own works – the last of them, the funeral cantata BWV 244a on the death of Leopold, a work which has sometimes been claimed as the original form of the *St Matthew Passion*.

Bach's secular superior: Prince Leopold of Anhalt-Köthen (1698–1728). *A gracious prince who both loved and knew music*. Anonymous painting

The prince, who had reigned since 1716, had long been a great lover of music. Even at the age of 12, when he was still Crown Prince, he persuaded his mother, then acting as regent, to appoint three court musicians for him, as if anticipating his founding of a Kapelle. When the Berlin court Kapelle was dissolved in 1713, Leopold took another step in that direction. He recruited a number of the members of this 'Stricker Kapelle', which he had known since attending the *Ritterakademie* in Berlin. By 1717, when he engaged Johann Sebastian Bach as Kapellmeister to succeed August Reinhard Stricker, who perhaps had not been quite up to the task, his ensemble was formed. It comprised 17 salaried musicians, one a clerk to copy out scores.[38]

At 400 thalers, Bach's annual salary was equal to that of the second-highest ranking official at court, the steward Gottlob von Nostitz. By comparison, towards the end of his time in Weimar he

The son of Christian Ferdinand Abel was Karl Friedrich Abel (1723–87). After studying the viola da gamba with his father, Karl Friedrich enrolled at the Thomasschule in Leipzig, before joining Pisendel's old orchestra in Dresden. After the marriage of George III to Charlotte of Mecklenburg, he became court musician in London, and from 1765 organised the famous 'Bach–Abel' concerts with Johann Christian Bach. He was a close friend of Thomas Gainsborough, who famously painted him. had been paid only 250 thalers, with smaller amounts as special fees. The Kapelle in Köthen was considerably larger than the Weimar, so working conditions were ideal. If, as has sometimes been conjectured, the prince played the viola da gamba himself it is not surprising that he engaged the most famous virtuoso on the cello and viola da gamba in the person of Christian Ferdinand Abel. In marked contrast to the Weimar Kapelle, most of the other instrumentalists were not mere ensemble players but proficient soloists on their respective instruments: violin, recorder, transverse flute, oboe, bassoon and perhaps trumpet. They must have been extremely capable musicians – indeed, how else could they have mastered the difficult passages of Bach's *Brandenburg Concerti*, suites and sonatas? Leopold obviously regarded the Kapelle as the jewel of his court,[39] and took its soloists with him not only on his regular visits to the spa at Karlsbad but, also, to the Dresden court, for instance in September 1719 to attend a wedding.

However, Bach did run into ecclesiastical obstructions in Köthen. Before he took up his post, he must have stopped to consider that the court was of the Calvinist and not Lutheran faith, meaning that he would have to forgo sacred music. This interrupted his career as virtuoso organist, and actually brought his main occupation to an end, although that would become apparent only later. Even sacred cantatas could be composed and performed only on special occasions. There is also the question of whether Bach had foreseen the problem of finding a suitable Lutheran school for his growing sons. In any case, he could not have guessed that he would be drawn into a violent dispute between the Reformed and the Lutheran factions.

The prince's mother, formerly the Duchess Regent Gisela Agnes, was Lutheran so there was a Lutheran community in the town of Köthen. It was small, but she was a zealous patroness, and Bach belonged to this society, as his intermittent attendance at Holy Communion shows. Despite the prince's tolerant nature, during Bach's Köthen period mother and son were at loggerheads over the increasing political influence of the Lutherans, especially among the landed gentry. Prince Leopold, seeing himself as hard pressed politically and financially, began to fight back, engaging in tactical manoeuvres and practising economies. It would seem that his treasured musical establishment had little to fear from these economic measures,[40] but in general Bach was torn. He was loyal to his Calvinist master but himself belonged to a Lutheran community that was in dispute with its prince – his employer.[41]

There are documentary records of a case illustrating Bach's unfortunate situation: his second marriage, to Anna Magdalena Wilcke, was celebrated in the Reformed church of the castle, not in the Lutheran church in town. Bach declined to make the dispensation payment due to the Lutheran community on this occasion, the large sum of 10 thalers, on the grounds that his wedding took place in the castle *by order of the prince*.[42] Presumably, he suffered from other such disputes. Perhaps it is no coincidence that on the title page of his first keyboard book for Anna Magdalena Bach, written in 1722, he noted down the titles of three works by the theologian August Pfeiffer: *Anti-Calvinismus*, *Evangelische Christenschule*, and *Antimelan-cholicus*.[43] Maybe Bach's interest in these three works, which were still in his library at the time of his death, suggests that he felt there was too much sectarian piety in Köthen, that he preferred to retreat into a more private sphere.

The documents that have been preserved reveal little of Bach's daily life in Köthen. He acted as godfather to several children, including the daughter of Abel the viola da gamba player, went to Holy Communion both with and without his wife, inherited a legacy of

224 thalers, went to Leipzig to examine an organ, to Berlin to take delivery of a new harpsichord, to Hamburg on professional business, and to the court of Schleitz to give a guest performance.

We do not know for certain exactly where he lived in the capital of the principality, a small town of only some 2,000 inhabitants at the time: it was probably at 11 Stiftstrasse, but may have been at 12 Holzmarkt. There are records of payments made to him by the court to recompense him for making his home available to the Kapelle for rehearsals. He must have been a strict taskmaster in that respect: in a petition of 1722, the Kantor of Köthen, Johann Jeremias Göbel, emphasises 'that even the most famous virtuosos rehearse and practise their music beforehand, as we may see clearly from the example of the princely Kapelle here, which practises its *exercitium musicum* every week'.

Bach conducted his ensemble from the violin or viola desk. Carl Philipp Emanuel has left us an account: 'He heard the slightest wrong note even in the largest combinations. As the greatest expert and judge of harmony, he liked best to play the viola, with appropriate loudness and softness. In his youth, and until the approach of old age, he played the violin cleanly and penetratingly, and thus kept the orchestra in better order than he could have done with the harpsichord. He understood to perfection the possibilities of all stringed instruments.'[44]

Further details of two musical journeys made by Bach are extant. The first, in the autumn of 1717, when he was still at Weimar but had already been appointed to Köthen, was to the court of Dresden, where he was to take part in an improvisation competition with the famous French keyboard virtuoso Louis Marchand. However, the Frenchman took fright at the last moment and left Dresden in the early morning by post coach. So Bach was left 'sole master of the scene of the contest', as the *Obituary* tells us.[45] He amazed the entire court by his playing, but was cheated out of the royal present of 500 thalers, over a year's salary by a dishonest servant.

This story has distinctly nationalistic overtones so perhaps it cannot be believed in every detail, but it is vouched for not only by the *Obituary* but also by a polemic in support of Bach by Magister Johann Abraham Birnbaum and published in 1739.[46] It does seem certain that Bach not only demonstrated his artistry at the Dresden court but kept his own eyes and ears open. At the time, Dresden's was by far the most important Kapelle in Germany, an ensemble which had adopted the newest, brilliant Italian style and, in addition, had a famous Italian opera company. If he really was in Dresden around this time, the new Kapellmeister of Köthen would have been anxious to glean ideas, to acquire sheet music and make contacts with the Dresden musicians. Analysing the compositions he subsequently wrote in Köthen, it can be assumed that not the least of his concerns was to study the many works of Vivaldi to be found among the stocks of music held in Dresden.[47]

The *Obituary* also describes another notable musical journey made by Bach: 'During this time, about the year 1722, he made a journey to Hamburg and was heard for more than two hours on the fine organ of the church of Catharinen-Kirche before the Magistrate and many other distinguished personages of the town, to general amazement. The aged Organist of this Church, Johann Adam Reinken, who at that time was nearly a hundred years old, listened to him with particular pleasure. Bach, at the request of those present, performed extempore the chorale *An Wasserflüssen Babylon* at great length (for almost a half-hour) and in different ways, just as the better organists of Hamburg used to do at the Saturday Vespers. On this, Reinken paid Bach the following compliment: "I thought that this art was dead, but I see that in you it still lives."'[48]

The incident described here probably took place in November 1720. Hamburg church records for that time mention Bach as a candidate for the post of organist at the city church of St Jacobi. We cannot now say whether he had decided to apply in advance or had made up his mind impulsively. In any case, the application fell through, since before the auditions were held Bach had 'to travel back to his Prince',[49] and, thus, was out of the running, leaving the way open for an applicant who, in the time-honoured Hanseatic style of buying offices, paid 4,000 marks into the church coffers on taking up his post.

Bach's notation: opening of the violin sonata BWV 1003, from the *Sei Solo a Violino senza Basso accompagnato*, in a clean copy of 1720. Bach, himself a violinist, seems to have transferred the curving movement of the string-player's arm directly to the appearance of the notation. It is unusual to find a composer's notation that is not just calligraphically perfect but even imparts something of the spirit of the music.

Years later, Johann Mattheson, in his journal *Der musikalische Patriot*, mentions the candidature of 'a certain great virtuoso' which came to nothing, and quotes with relish from the Christmas sermon preached at the time by the chief pastor of Hamburg, the cantata librettist Erdmann Neumeister: 'He was firmly convinced that even if one of the angels should come down from Heaven, one who played divinely and wished to become organist of St Jacobi but had no money, he might just as well fly away again.'[50] In further publications, Mattheson describes two works that Bach probably played at his performance in Hamburg: the *Fantasia* and *Fugue in G minor* BWV 542, and the cantata BWV 21. While he praised the organ composition,[51] he criticised the cantata, chiefly for the unnatural treatment of the text (*Ich, ich, ich, ich hatte viel Bekümmernis . . . – I, I, I, I was in great distress . . .*).[52] The interesting point of the whole affair is the degree of respect openly shown: apparently the educated public of the time was already interested in discussions on music that helped to form opinion and determine norms.

Bach manuscripts, such as the one on the facing page, are rarely exhibited in public today. The ink has corroded, leaving the substance of the paper in a dangerously fragile state. To preserve these valuable manuscripts, attempts have been made to neutralise the acids that are being discharged. There are also experiments in splitting the written sheets to place a layer of paper between the back and front sides.

Whatever the accuracy of detail in these accounts of Bach's appearances in Dresden and Hamburg, he was obviously a renowned virtuoso on both harpsichord and organ, and a stylistically versatile performer to boot. Who but Bach was master of both the dying tradition of north German organ music and the modern keyboard playing in the French and Italian style? The demands Bach made in Köthen on the harpsichord are evident in some of the works written there, not least the fifth *Brandenburg Concerto*. When the keyboard part of his work was extended in the final, 1721 version, it became, in a way, the first virtuouso concerto for keyboard and orchestra even though this is still, to a degree, concertante chamber music. By comparison, the *Chromatic Fantasia* BWV 903, composed at the same time, perhaps as a *tombeau* for Maria Barbara, in which the composer is apparently improvising rhapsodically on his instrument, seems positively modern.[53]

It is not known if Bach seriously hoped to move to Hamburg in 1720. But just as certainly as he was exploring new terrain there, he also dedicated the *Brandenburg Concerti* to Margrave Christian Ludwig of Brandenburg, with an eye to making useful contacts. In his dedication of 24 March 1721, he recollects casually that *a couple of years ago* the margrave was asking him for new compositions. Was this a hint at a wish for another post, or was it just another sign that Bach, always independent, preferred to keep his options open?

The death of Maria Barbara during his Köthen period marked a watershed in his life. She was buried on 7 July 1720. Whether Bach was really away with the prince visiting a spa when she died, as the *Obituary* states, cannot be confirmed. In any case, not unusually for his time, he was very soon looking for a second wife. On 3 December 1721, he married Anna Magdalena Wilcke, then 20 years old, daughter of the court trumpeter of Weissenfels, Johann Caspar Wilcke. The first record of her presence in Köthen dates from two months earlier, when she is mentioned as a 'princely singer'. Considering Bach's strong links with Weissenfels, he could well have recruited his future wife for the Köthen ensemble himself. Whether the wedding celebrations in Bach's house were quiet, as might be expected of a second marriage, or whether Rhine wine flowed freely we do not know, but Bach's wine bills for this time came to the remarkably high sum of 27 thalers.

It was not part of Bach's job at Köthen to compose much vocal music. Perhaps he was required to perform a sacred or secular cantata for New Year's Day and another for the prince's birthday. Only two of these works are extant: BWV 134a, *Die Zeit, die Tag und Jahre macht* (*The time that makes the day and year*), and BWV 173a, *Durchlauchtster Leopold* (*Most Serene Leopold*). The texts of half a dozen more have been preserved, or can be more or less reconstructed from later revisions; in addition, there are a few works whose origin is not clear.⁵⁴ The texts of most of the Köthen cantatas are by Christian Friedrich Hunold, a poet who followed the *galant* style and was known chiefly for his opera librettos and Passion texts. At the time, Hunold was working and living in nearby Halle. Bach probably knew him personally.

Even if other occasional compositions were commissioned for Köthen, there can be no doubt that during the five-year period when he was Kapellmeister, Bach concentrated on writing instrumental music. While a whole series of instrumental works may have been lost, those written at this time that have survived, including concerti, orchestral suites, sonatas and the keyboard cycle, present a very rounded impression of the Köthen Bach.

About 20 instrumental concerti are assumed to have been written at this time: they include, as well as the six *Brandenburg Concerti* BWV 1046–1051, the two violin concerti, BWV 1041 in A minor, and BWV 1042 in E major, and the 'double' violin concerto BWV 1043. Other works can be more or less plausibly reconstructed entirely from their later keyboard concerto versions, for instance the violin concerti BWV 1052a and 1056a, the oboe d'amore concerto BWV 1055a, the oboe and violin concerto BWV 1060, and the concerto for three violins BWV 1064R.

By comparison with the corpus of Antonio Vivaldi, who is generally regarded as one of the fathers of the modern solo concerto and was probably an example to Bach, Bach's extant concerti reveal clear differences. Vivaldi, in common with other Italian composers of his generation, perfected a concerto form notable for its concision, tuneful nature and brilliance. With the publication of *L'estro armonico* in 1711, Vivaldi opened his campaign for the concerto grosso. The work appeared, like the violin sonatas Op 1 and Op 2, in which Vivaldi was sounding out the ground, in many editions published in Amsterdam, London and Paris. The Vivaldian concerto became an autonomous entity redefining an entire genre, almost like the *da capo* of the contemporaneous aria.

Vivaldi published mainly violin concerti; he composed well over 200 of them. Only violin performance seemed sufficiently popular to him, well-developed enough in terms of virtuosity to attract a wide audience. He did write concerti for other instruments but seldom had them printed, so as not to confuse the still 'inexperienced' public.

Not so with Bach. Even in view of the uncertainty of the source material, it can be said confidently that he wrote very much less. While he certainly studied the appealing and indeed persuasive ideas of Vivaldi, he made limited use of them. He did not create any supra-regional school but remained apart from the European scene as a whole, and hesitated to publish his music at all. Bach was not a man to take the smooth and easy path. It is not coincidental but symptomatic that it is difficult to determine how the different versions of even his instrumental ensemble music have come down to us. Apparently, Bach spent many years on the same few works, and quite often neither the beginning nor the end of that work-process can be traced.

One may, therefore, speak of 'work in progress' in two senses: first, he continued to develop his musical ideas and innovations in one and the same composition; and second, he revised his works with a view to changes in external circumstances. Such a procedure was something new in musical history. Of course, there had always been adaptations and rearrangements, but the usual practice was to create new works at new phases of the composer's career and for new conditions of performance or demands of patrons. Even as thoughtful a composer as Heinrich Schütz illustrates this approach: one work reflects his time of study with Giovanni Gabrieli, another his interest in Claudio Monteverdi, a third his concern with German traditions, and so on.

Bach's method was different. To him, the writing of music was not merely the creation of new compositions but the retelling of old ground, revisiting earlier works. From this viewpoint, composition became a matter of working on problems that were no longer just those of craftsmanship or taste, or of ability or the lack of it, of being right or wrong but the search for the one and only truth. Depending on the way we look at it, this idea either points back to the Middle Ages or forward to Beethoven and Schoenberg.

To return to Bach's instrumental concerti, truth cannot be a case of making *one* instrumental sound or *one* form absolute. Accordingly, Bach wrote more concerti for a varied ensemble of soloists, especially string players, than for individual soloists. A motley collection of soloists features in the *Brandenburg Concerti*: the first has two horns, three oboes and a piccolo-violin; the second, trumpet, recorder, oboe and violin; the sixth, low-pitched stringed instruments, which normally take a less prominent place; while in the third, all ten string players are soloists. With such musical ideas, Bach reveals his grounding in the traditions of the music of the town pipers as well as the organ, with its characteristic sound and the colourful use of the *Mixtur* stops.[55] At the same time, the use of such forces ensures the polyphonic effect which he pursued above all; in contrast to Vivaldi's work, the *Brandenburg Concerti* do not have soloists and string ensemble players but employ a variety of ways to use the separate voices as solos, in small groups or in a *tutti* effect, thus allowing them to alternate their functions.

It was only hesitantly and never with full commitment that Bach adopted the Vivaldian formal pattern, which can typically be described as a sequence of ritornello – solo passage 1 – ritornello – solo passage 2 – ritornello – solo passage 3 – ritornello, and so on. As the early versions of the first, third and sixth *Brandenburg Concerti* show, he was initially much closer to the old German ideal of chamber music-making, intended more for personal pleasure in performance with a *Collegium Musicum* than for the gratification of a concert audience at a virtuoso performance. Whether the works mentioned or early versions of them were written before Bach's organ and keyboard transcriptions of Vivaldi concerti in the years 1713–14, whether they were written in Weimar at all or not until the early part of his Köthen period,[56] they clearly show Bach to have been a complex thinker: a traditionalist in preserving old notions of musical genres, but a precursor of Viennese classicism in the amount of development involved.

The *Brandenburg Concerti* Nos 2, 4 and 5, which belong to a later phase, differ only to a qualified extent: there is no longer a ritornello opening section introduced immediately, as in the sixth concerto, but the ritornello of the opening movement of the fourth concerto is so long, with 83 bars, and so subtly differentiated in the interplay of its concertante group that it can hardly be called a ritornello any more, and certainly not a 'theme'.

The semantic factor inherent in this purely instrumental music is new and significant. The early version of the first *Brandenburg Concerto* BWV 1046, which was very likely to have been composed as an overture to the *Hunt Cantata* BWV 208 or written for a later performance in 1716, is clearly a programmatic composition, even if there are no explanatory sonnets such as in the case of Vivaldi's *The Four Seasons*. The horn players are heard blowing their 'signals' in the first movement while huntsmen call and dogs bark. In this case there could be programmatic meaning in the fact that the introductory ritornello, with its 13 bars, is irregular and asymmetrical, representing the confusion of an opening scene, also expressed in the fact that the opening bar is a kind of trill which the composition, confounding our expectations, then takes no further, as if it were only in the nature of a signal or even a leitmotif. The lament of the oboe which dominates the second movement, imitating the human voice and extremely expressive, has recently even been interpreted as showing Bach's sympathy with the suffering of the poor hunted animals.[57]

The semantic factor, however, is not exhausted in this programmatic element. Perhaps more important is a specific concept of instrumental ensemble writing in general. It is used as the organ of a tonal language, combining the two traditional structural elements of imitation and dance-like figuration, and then leaving them behind. One can now listen to instrumental music as a procedural experience in the same way as vocal music. Such formally different structures as the opening movements of the first and fifth *Brandenburg Concerti* are linked in this sense by a dramatic factor, not unlike the changing fortunes represented in drama itself.[58] Among Bach's slow movements, not least those of the violin concerti, some are expansive and song-like, speaking of supernatural peace, reminding the listener of great poetry. It would be worth studying how far Bach may have kept to the formal rules of rhetoric in constructing his concerto movements, and indeed an attempt has recently been made to do so using the third *Brandenburg Concerto* as an illustration.[59]

Sire: Since I had the happiness, a few years ago, to play by command before your Royal Highness, and observed at that time that you derived some pleasure from the small musical talent that Heaven has given me; and since, when I was taking leave of Your Royal Highness, you did me the honour to request that I send you some of my compositions . . . begging you not to judge their imperfection by the strict measure of the refined and delicate taste that everyone knows that you possess, but rather to consider kindly the deep respect and the most humble obedience which I am thereby attempting to show you.
From Bach's Dedication of the *Brandenburg Concerti* to the margrave

The autograph dedication of the *Brandenburg Concerti* shows clearly that at the time, in 1721, Bach must have had some trouble assembling six suitable works from his extant stock of compositions; there are obvious traces of revision and rearrangement. Why, if he was short of ensemble concerti, did he not resort to one of the violin concerti that may well have been in existence at this time? Admittedly, they are more strikingly similar to Vivaldi's concerti in form and thematic material than the *Brandenburg Concerti*. Perhaps Bach wanted to present concertante music in a particularly 'German' style in the *Brandenburg Concerti*, a style depending more

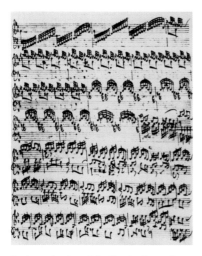

An important contribution to the early history of the keyboard concerto: the cadenza from the first movement of the fifth *Brandenburg Concerto* in Bach's manuscript, probably written in 1721.

on complex tonal colour than on smooth Italianate elegance, appealing to connoisseurs who could appreciate both the history of the genre and the specific difference between the various works concerned?

On the other hand, Bach was entirely in line with the courtly taste of his time in the four orchestral suites traditionally known as overtures, BWV 1066–1069. For all their skill and subtlety of detail, he is unusually conventional both in his treatment of the expansive style of the French overture and in developing the ensuing *divertissement* or dance sequence; this is 'feudal' music of the kind that came from the court of France's Louis XIV. The playful flute of the B-minor overture can hardly prevail against the trumpets and kettledrums in the two D-major overtures.

Of Bach's sonatas and suites for melodic instruments, some were composed in Weimar, while usually others are ascribed to the Leipzig period,[60] including the majority of the extant lute compositions and the flute sonatas BWV 1030 and 1032. (The trio sonata from the *Musical Offering* BWV 1079 was certainly written in Leipzig.) Hypothetical datings, however, are never without their attendant problems, since Bach revised his sonatas repeatedly or transcribed them for other instruments, making it difficult to identify and date the original versions. It is striking that when approaching the sonata Bach initially wrote works for two melodic instruments and basso continuo, that is, traditional trio sonatas, but then tended increasingly to replace one of the two melodic instruments with the right-hand part on the harpsichord. This may have been for practical reasons: such works entailed less expense to perform, needing only one soloist with Bach himself playing obbligato harpsichord.

Besides the sonatas for flute BWV 1035, viola da gamba BWV 1027–1029, and violin BWV 1014–1019, which cannot be reliably dated, the works of the Köthen period certainly include three sequences which have brought Bach his most lasting renown in this field: the three sonatas and three partitas for solo violin BWV 1001–1006, the six suites for solo cello BWV 1007–1012; and the unspecified partita BWV 1013, usually played on the flute. The violin solos are dated 1720 and have come down to us in an autographed manuscript described as *Libro primo*; the existence of other solo works for cello and flute suggests that Bach had a series of works for violin in mind.

Early on, Bach's solos for violin and cello were regarded as miracles of both intellect and virtuosity, a fact noted by two of his very different admirers. In his biography of Bach, published in 1802, Johann Nikolaus Forkel wrote:

'How far Bach's deliberation and perspicacity went in the handling of melody and harmony, and how far he was inclined to exhaust all the possibilities of both, is also evident in his endeavour to arrange a single melody in such a way that no other singable part could be sung or set against it.'[61]

Johann Nikolaus Forkel (1749–1818) was the son of a cobbler and, like Bach, a chorister at Lüneberg. He studied law in Göttingen, where he became music director in 1776. As a music theorist, he was an autodidact, heavily influenced by Mattheson's *Der volkomme Capellmeister*. In 1802, he published the first full biography of Bach, based on material supplied by Bach's sons. Following the death of C P E Bach, he unsuccessfully applied for the music director of five churches in Hamburg. He was also a composer, though his compositions have disappeared from the concert hall. His *Allgemeine Geschichte der Musik* was the first German attempt at writing a systematic history of music.

In an 1877 letter to Clara Schumann, Johannes Brahms commented:

'To my mind, the chaconne is one of the most wonderful and mysterious pieces in all music. Using a system [of notes] for a small instrument, the man composes a whole world of the most profound ideas and powerful feelings.'[62]

Bach did all he could to follow his organic principle consistently; he made the individual musician absolute, conducting a dialogue with himself. He was less concerned with the development of linear free-floating monophony than with proving that a single melodic instrument can be handled polyphonically and fugally. It becomes clear how much 'concentrated polyphony' there is in a movement such as the famous chaconne from the violin partita in D minor, BWV 1004, if his arrangement is compared to one of the more elaborate arrangements of it made by Felix Mendelssohn-Bartholdy, Robert Schumann, Johannes Brahms or Ferruccio Busoni.

In 1717, Prince Leopold appointed his Kapellmeister Bach as director of chamber music, indicating that such music played an important part in Köthen. This is not surprising given the prince's alleged fondness for the viola da gamba, the elevated chamber instrument *par excellence*. Nor is it surprising that a relatively large number of Bach's chamber music works from the Köthen period have been preserved.

Bach also evinces a particular liking for keyboard composition, which cannot be directly connected with his professional duties. It was in Köthen that he wrote the French and English suites BWV 812–817 and BWV 806–811, the *Chromatic Fantasia* BWV 903, the two-part *Inventions* and three-part *Sinfonias* BWV 772–801, and the first part of the *Well-Tempered Clavier* BWV 846–869.

In view of Bach's disappointments with the professional and religious environment in Köthen, this kind of composition may mark a retreat into private life. However, the subject might also be seen from an opposite viewpoint: in Köthen, Bach had a genuinely *gracious* prince who loved and appreciated music, enabling him to follow his inner dynamic to conquer new territory in the realm of his art, regardless of his professional career. If all we had from the Köthen period was keyboard works such as the suites and the

Chromatic Fantasia, that new territory would relate to the keyboard alone, but such a view would not cover the two-part *Inventions*, the three-part *Sinfonias* and the *Well-Tempered Clavier*. Admittedly, these works were also written for harpsichord, but they show a musical approach of such universal validity that it goes far beyond concern with just one particular instrument.

Yet all this began in a very modest way: Bach drew up a work intended for teaching his son Wilhelm Friedemann, who was just nine at the time, and revealing his enthusiasm as a teacher, inscribed its title page: *Clavier-Büchlein. Vor Wilhelm Friedemann Bach, angefangen in Cöthen den 22. Januarij Anno. 1720* (*Little Keyboard Book, for Wilhelm Friedemann Bach, begun in Köthen on 22 January of the year 1720*). Wilhelm Friedemann was obviously not to get the kind of teaching that Johann Sebastian had received at the same age from his own brother in Ohrdruf; he was not to learn from the example of others in the apprenticeship tradition of organists. Bach wanted his eldest son to have an organised, systematic introduction to music, so he personally composed the examples the boy would need.

The core of the *Clavier-Büchlein*, therefore, consists of about a dozen preludes similar to those in the *Well-Tempered Clavier*, on which Bach was just beginning to work at the time, and the *Inventions* and *Sinfonias* probably written especially for his son. It also contains chorales perhaps included with didactic intent: *Wer nur den lieben Gott lässt walten* (*He who lets the Lord alone decide*); *Jesu, meine Freude* (*Jesus, my joy*); and various dance movements by other composers. Bach's systematic approach is obvious from the title pages which, perhaps with a view to possible publication, he removed from the *Clavier-Büchlein*, completed and added to the clean copies of the works mentioned above:

An Honest Method whereby lovers of the keyboard, and particularly those anxious to learn it, are shown the clear way not merely (1) to learn to play well in two parts, but also, having made further progress (2) to proceed well and correctly with three obbligato parts, and also not only to have good inventions

TEACHER TO HIS SONS

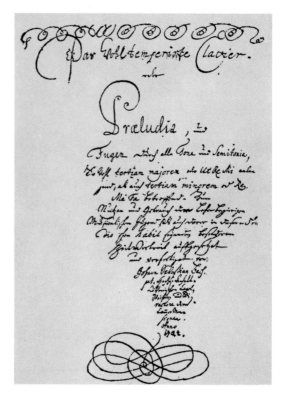

For the use and profit of musical youth that is anxious to learn: autograph title page of the *Well-Tempered Clavier*, 1722.

but to develop them properly, and most of all to acquire a singing manner of playing, as well as a strong foretaste of composition. Made by Joh. Seb. Bach, Kapellmeister to His Princely Highness of Köthen.

The Well-Tempered Clavier, or Preludes and Fugues through all the tones and semitones, regarding both the tertia major or Ut Re Mi, and the tertia minor or Re Mi Fa. For the use and profit of musical youth that is anxious to learn, and for those who, being already experienced in that study, wish for pastime, set down and prepared by Johann Sebastian Bach, Kapellmeister to His Princely Highness of Anhalt-Köthen, and director of his chamber music. Anno 1722.

Although the educational intent was similar, Bach placed more emphasis on the *Inventions* or *Sinfonias* than on the *Well-Tempered*

Clavier. The *Inventions* or *Sinfonias* show how an idea (*inventio*) can become not just 'pure', that is harmonious, through development (by *elaboratio*) but becomes a small composition in itself, for which a *singing manner* of playing on the keyboard is required. The statement that the pattern of composition must be not just structurally well developed but also *singing* can also be summed up in the terms of traditional compositional theory: a composition should not only show mastery of the rules of strict counterpoint but be artistic in its use of musical rhetoric and poetics. Recent commentators have used these easily understood little pieces not just to penetrate the 'mysteries' of Bach's counterpoint but also to work out the emotional, figurative, representational and symbolical elements in them. Later works of strict counterpoint like the *Art of Fugue* and the *Musical Offering* have been studied for their rhetorical factors, not without arousing some controversy among scholars.[63]

Bach's spiritual superior: Salomon Deyling (1677–1755), Superintendent of Leipzig. A stern character with whom Bach had many disputes. Anonymous painting

In the preludes in F-sharp minor and A major from the first part of the *Well-Tempered Clavier,* Bach took up the genre of the 'invention', but generally he is concerned with something greater: the work is conceived, not from the point of view of the *performer* who is to be introduced to the world of music, but in relation to the *music,* which reveals a part of its universal nature. The circuitous manner in which Bach sets out his ideas on the title page, using the terminology of the old note names (ut-re-mi-fa-sol-la), may conceal his excitement at this new project. After all, the idea of a series designed to consist of a prelude and fugue for each of the 24 keys of the 12-tone scale was something new at the time. Earlier, Johann Pachelbel, Johann Kuhnau and Johann Caspar Ferdinand Fischer had written keyboard cycles arranged by key, some of them quite extensive, but these were primarily concerned with the practical question of how far a player on a keyboard instrument tuned to 'mean-tone temperament' could venture into remote keys.

'Venture' is an applicable word because in Bach's time it was unusual to tune to 'equal temperament', where the octave is rigorously divided into 12 equal semitones. With the help of this procedure it is certainly possible to play the harpsichord in all keys and modulate it without having to retune from case to case, but one is intervening considerably in what was assumed at the time to be the God-given natural order, whereby each key with its pure intervals deriving from the overtones forms a system in itself, harmonising with the other systems only to a limited extent. Compromises were included in the field of 'mean-tone' tuning, according to the maxim that there were some pure intervals in the nature of music, some moderately impure for the sake of compositional progress in modulation.

As a practical musician, Bach himself lived with such compromises. As the confident creator of

Until the 1950s, there was no doubt that the tuning system Bach had in mind for his *Well Tempered Clavier* was 'equal temperament', which divides the octave into 12 semitones of equal size. In no source does Bach ever comment on tuning issues and it was only with the renewed interest in historic temperaments during the last five decades of the 20th century that questions were raised if equal temperament really was the tuning system that Bach had wanted. However, after a prolonged period of confusion, close study of secondary sources and external evidence, it became clear that Bach favoured equal temperament, or at least a tuning system that is extremely close to equal temperament.

the *Well-Tempered Clavier* he worked out, quite clearly, the contradiction in the nature of the subject: a modern composer who wanted to explore the realm of music in every direction must make his own laws and be ready, instead of using the simple numerical series denoting the oscillating relationships of the overtone series 1:2:3:4:5, and so on, to turn to the irrational number $\sqrt{2}$ in order to divide the octave, with strict rationality, into 12 equal but no longer 'natural' semitones. The mere fact that Bach tackled this problem makes the *Well-Tempered Clavier* a seminal work of western music tackling a fundamental, metaphysical problem: was man to pursue his art within the framework of natural order, or might he keep devising and applying new laws in the further development of his musical material outside the divine laws of nature?

Bach, as always, went his own way, answering the question according to the tonal system that suited his profound thinking and wide-ranging creativity in the spirit of progress, of the universal formula. But in so doing he did not open the door to compulsively regulated composition, nor to individual and random writing of the kind to be found in the avant-garde music of the late 20th century. Rather he gave his music historically, socially, emotionally and stylistically identifiable features of vitality and great diversity. The preludes and fugues of the *Well-Tempered Clavier* are based on a wealth of characteristic traditions of genre and form, of specific styles and idioms of musical language. Mozart, Beethoven, Schubert, Schumann, Felix and Fanny Mendelssohn-Bartholdy, Brahms, Wagner, Hindemith and many others after them all identified with the world of the *Well-Tempered Clavier*, sometimes with astonishing intensity. Above all, this identification arises from that work's very ambivalence; it represents a strict system, and at the same time invites us to make discoveries of a fantastic and sensuous nature.

Kantor of St Thomas's:
Bach's early Leipzig period
1723–1729

When the Leipzig city council met on 9 April 1723 to discuss
the appointment of a new Kantor to the church of St Thomas's –
and more importantly, a list of candidates headed by Bach – Appeals
Councillor Abraham Christoph Platz said that '[. . .] since the
best man could not be obtained, mediocre ones would have to be
accepted'.[64]

An equally famous quote can be found in a letter that Bach wrote
years later, on 28 October 1730, in which he intimates to the friend
of his youth, Georg Erdmann in Danzig, that he would be more
than ready to give up the post of Kantor, adding that: *At first, indeed,
it did not seem at all proper to me to change my position of Kapellmeister
for that of Kantor.*[65] Read and interpreted in their wider context, these
two remarks throw a spotlight on the general cultural politics of
Leipzig and on Bach's personal situation when he took up his
new position.[66]

In the first half of the 18th century, Leipzig was in a state of
flux, showing a 'Janus face' of tradition and progress. A 1710 guide
to church services was entitled *Leipziger Kirchen-Staat* (*Leipzig, State
of Churches*); the more modern-minded Leipzig was described as
'Little Paris' or 'Athens on the Pleisse'. The city, the site of one of the
oldest universities in Germany, had played an important part in
the history of orthodox Lutheranism, and was governed with a
firm hand by its council. In 1716, a decree was issued 'against the
frivolous conduct prevalent in coffee houses'; since these were
places where citizens met for discussions on progressive subjects,

a strict eye was kept on them. That year, another decree ordained that 'the professors and others who lecture here at the university should avoid all suspect opinions and new ways of speaking and writing'. The ban on students 'going about the streets in night-caps and night-shirts'[67] is rather more amusing than the draconian censorship imposed on literary works and theatre.

But at the turn of the century, Leipzig, with a population of 15,700, was also a flourishing centre of commerce and trade fairs, and had already overtaken Nuremberg and Frankfurt as a commercial centre. The growing power of the middle class was ever more evident in the magnificent Baroque palaces built as private houses or business premises in the early 18th century, particularly on the initiative of the young mayor Franz Conrad Romanus. Leipzig had always been well known for its book trade and was increasingly a centre of Enlighten-ment literature and drama. It was here, in 1731, that Gottsched presented his play *Der sterbende Cato* (*The Dying Cato*), and in 1748, Gotthold Ephraim Lessing's first drama, *Der junge Gelehrte* (*The Young Scholar*) was produced. When Goethe came to study in Leipzig in 1765 it was regarded as the intellectual metropolis of Germany.

There were also two aspects to the musical life of the city. First, the church and municipal music emphasising tradition and reli-gious observance that was most prominently represented by the Kantors of St Thomas's. For centuries, they had been musicians and composers highly regarded beyond Leipzig itself; a number were outstanding scholars. The list of holders of the office before Bach reads like an honour roll of German musical history: Sethus Calvisius, Johann Hermann Schein, Tobias Michael, Sebastian Knüpfer, Johann Schelle, Johann Kuhnau. In contrast to many other cities, the Kantor still held third place in the hierarchy of St Thomas's School, after the Rektor (headmaster) and the Konrektor (second master), taking precedence over the Tertius (third master). Such status carried with it a duty of preserving continuity and cultivating tradition: motets from the time of the Reformation were still being

The scene of Bach's work for so many years: the interior of St Thomas's church in Leipzig before its restoration in 1885. The organ loft is visible above left. Engraving by O Kutschera from a watercolour by Hubert Kratz

sung in the Leipzig churches in Bach's time, and the fashionable new Italian style was allowed in the main churches of St Thomas and St Nikolai during divine service only with special permission.

Bach's predecessor generally observed the express instruction that the Kantor was not to compose in too 'operatic a style', and must do his best to keep his cantatas and *Passions* free of *secco* recitatives and da capo arias of too secular a nature. In 1709, he specifically forswore 'the madrigal style'.[68] Traditionally, church music was to be correctly composed and expertly performed, but should also confine itself to subordinate functions, of serving the glory of God and for human edification. Intriguing new sounds and indeed the very enjoyment of music for its own sake were considered suspect in the secular area, and banned entirely from church use.

But as a musical city, Leipzig boasted a second face: it had its own opera company, albeit only from 1693 to 1720. Modern sacred music was played in at least one church. The opera company performed only during the three annual trade fairs, and was clearly designed to appeal to the pockets and musical interests of outside visitors. Since it could not afford to pay a large number of professional musicians, most of the performers were university students. In 1702, the opera was even directed by a student: Georg Philipp Telemann, then just 21 years old and a protégé of Mayor Romanus, who was not much older himself. He had been so impressed by Telemann's setting of the 6th Psalm that he immediately commissioned him to compose church music for St Thomas's, taking turns with the Kantor, Johann Kuhnau, who had only just been appointed to the post but was seen from the first to be an ailing man who could not produce much music.

As the new star of Leipzig's musical firmament, Telemann also became music director of the *Neukirche*, a building that had fallen into disrepair over the centuries but had been brought back into use in 1699 for church services at the request of the city merchants. Telemann had to agree to step down as director of the opera company, but although he complied formally with this stipulation he continued to rely on the student *Collegium Musicum* which he had founded, and which formed the nucleus of the orchestra for the opera.

Although Telemann soon left Leipzig, the *Neukirche* continued to be the home of modern church music, taking its tone from the Italian concertante and operatic style; the first oratorio-like Passion to be performed in Leipzig was given there. Some regarded it as a farce, others as a feast for the ears. In 1720, Kuhnau, complained in a petition that he could no longer get suitable musicians for his music in the church, since the musical students had fallen for the lures of 'the wild, operatic kind of music' performed in the *Neukirche*. They had, he said, little idea 'of the true church style, which requires a long and particular period of study'.[69]

Johann Kuhnau (1660–1722), Bach's predecessor in Leipzig, should not be underestimated. Although his health was poor, he was not a good teacher, and he resisted the idea of too operatic an element in the city's church music, by traditional standards he was far better educated than the self-made Bach. In 1688, he published a doctoral thesis on the legal conditions affecting church musicians, and in 1700 he produced a satirical novel, *Der musikalische Quacksalber (The Musical Quack)*. Significantly, his various writings and editions of keyboard music meant he was more popular with the public than Bach was with the four parts of the *Klavierübung*.

The success of modern music at the *Neukirche* expressed the desire of the ambitious middle class to have access to the music that had hitherto been a privilege of the nobility. Music was no longer to be performed and heard only in the context of the church and social order, but to be experienced as an autonomous aesthetic phenomenon, providing the senses with immediate pleasure. At first, however, the middle class did not have the institutional and financial resources of a court, nor did their work ethic allow them to approve of pure pleasure as enjoyed by the indolent nobility. Consequently, the cultivation of the new kind of music within the church was a case of making a virtue of necessity.

The citizens of Leipzig did not encounter hostility from the nobility in aspiring to their own cultural values. Indeed, the youthful Mayor Romanus, a protégé of the Elector of Dresden, had been specifically appointed to make Leipzig a modern city, quite possibly in the face of conservative opposition. A few weeks after he took office, the city council received a decree from Dresden clearly inspired by the forceful mayor (who, incidentally, was soon toppled from the post). In plain language, it proposed an extensive series of innovations: sluicing down the streets, fixing street lights to buildings, the introduction of shooting practice, checking up on the coffee houses. Furthermore, 'because gentlemen from outside the city are always visiting Leipzig, particularly during the fairs, music in the civic churches should be in a good state.'[70]

The make-up of the city council, which unanimously appointed Bach as Kantor of St Thomas's on 22 April 1723, reflected the state of cultural policy in Leipzig. There were certain traditionalists who did not want an outstanding artist as Kantor, any more than they wanted the new style of operatic music to be performed in the church. They thought the new Kantor should concentrate on his traditional duties, which marked him out primarily as a teacher. When, the more conservative councillors must have sighed, would they get another Kantor able to maintain discipline and order among the choirboys, a Kantor who would teach Latin to the lower classes in the school? But there were also innovators on the council who would rather have kept the offices of Kantor of St Thomas's and Music Director of the city separate, and who wanted an outstanding artistic personality for the latter job.

These innovators were either in the majority on the council or skilful tacticians, and even seem to have issued carefully calculated press releases in pursuit of their aims. By such means they succeeded in eliminating a number of candidates of only average talents, and they finally presented the council as a whole with a shortlist of four men. These four candidates, regarded as outstanding or even unsurpassed in their field, were Georg Philipp Telemann, Johann Friedrich Fasch, Christoph Graupner and Johann Sebastian Bach. It is hardly surprising that Telemann, who had already been very successful in Leipzig, was the first and initially the only choice. But once he had negotiated a rise in his salary as Kantor of the Johanneum in Hamburg and Music Director of the main churches,

Telemann turned down the Leipzig appointment. The court Kapellmeisters Fasch and Graupner, both of them also 'old Leipzig men' and scholars, were then invited to audition, but they could not get permission to leave their respective posts at the courts of Zerbst and Darmstadt. So Bach had his chance without 'losing' to any of the other three: the council's invitations to Telemann and Fasch preceded the arrival of his own application, which for unknown reasons came in very late, and there was no final contest between him and Graupner, who had already withdrawn.

Bach auditioned for the post of Kantor in the church of St Thomas's on 7 February 1723. Study of the sources supports the conjecture that on this Quinquagesima Sunday he, like other candidates, performed two cantatas. Although we cannot now reconstruct in detail any stipulations about the choice of text and musical style made by the council, it is obvious that Bach's tactics were well judged: before the sermon he performed BWV 22, *Jesus nahm sich* (*Jesus took unto him*), a standard Sunday cantata beginning with a Biblical text, ending in a simple chorale movement with instrumental accompaniment in the central German tradition – in general, not presenting the people of Leipzig with anything too new or unusual. The conservative councillors probably nodded approvingly.

After the sermon, came the cantata BWV 23, *Du wahrer Gott und Davids Sohn* (*Thou true God and son of David*), an exquisite piece of sacred chamber music full of bold technical and harmonic elements, showing Bach very much the skilled Kapellmeister of Köthen. The chorale element is not so much explicitly presented as concealed in the recitative-like central section of this originally three-movement work, and takes the shape of a purely instrumental passage. But as a cantata without a final chorale may still have been frowned upon at St Thomas's, Bach seems to have been advised to add one to his work. He probably took the skilfully polyphonic chorale arrangement on *Christe, du Lamm Gottes* (*Christ, thou Lamb of God*) from the music he had to hand, at the last minute adding it as a new

The little domain of the Kantor of St Thomas's: the church and school of St Thomas in Leipzig. A group of black-clad choirboys is walking to church from the school, which also contained Bach's lodgings. Engraving by Johann Gottfried Krügner the Elder, 1723

closing movement, admittedly distorting the original proportions.

Even Appeals Councillor Abraham Christoph Platz finally voted for Bach; his disparaging comment on the necessity of falling back on 'mediocre' applicants turned out, on closer study of the minutes of the meeting, to have been a last-minute tactical manoeuvre in order to bring another musician into the running, who would make a biddable Kantor, 'a man in Pirna'. In fact, he was not referring to Bach. Indeed, Platz mentioned Bach's 'good reputation', and it was not him but a colleague, Adrian Steger, another member of the conservative group, who told the new Kantor to ensure that his compositions 'were not theatrical'. It was emphasised several times in council meetings that Bach was to teach the lower classes in the school or arrange for a suitable substitute. Both points emerge again in the contract signed by Bach, which required him 'to preserve the good order in the churches, [and] so arrange the music that it shall not last too long, and it shall be of such a nature as not to make an operatic impression, but rather incite the listeners to devotion.'[71]

CHRIST, THOU LAMB OF GOD

Can it really have been as hard for Bach as he implies in his letter of October 1730 to Georg Erdmann to exchange the office of Kapellmeister at Köthen for that of the Kantor of St Thomas's and Music Director of Leipzig? At the time, he claims the reason for the move not as professional advancement but because his sovereign's musical interests had become *somewhat lukewarm*, as well as the prince's marriage to an unmusical wife, the prospect of a higher salary, and better educational opportunities for his sons. Perhaps the climate of the court at Köthen was not, in fact, as good as Bach could have wished any longer. Perhaps the *unmusical* wife, although Bach had been obliged to suffer her for only just over a year, really did not appreciate the elevated musical tastes of the composer. Perhaps Bach wanted to secure his future, and that of his sons, by taking up a lifetime post in a university city.

Although Bach's position may have come to disappoint him, at first it must have been very stimulating. The city councillors who had backed him could not entirely free him of the more onerous duties of a Kantor, but tended to regard his post of 'director musices' as resembling that of a modern Kapellmeister. Two connected factors may have drawn Bach to Leipzig: his unshakeable religious faith, which attracted him to a church position; and his strong desire to set new standards in musical composition. Bach had the chance to combine his experiences as church musician and Kapellmeister in one of the most highly regarded musical posts anywhere in Germany, to bring the courtly tone and modern style to the middle classes, and in so doing to work on the creation of great music.

Seen in this light, the *St John* and *St Matthew Passions* are still improperly described as bourgeois works of art with their roots in sacred music which at the same time opened the door to the concertante music of ideas. It was only thanks to the strenuous efforts of influential citizens of Leipzig that Bach could compose or perform the *Passions* at all, since the only music in that genre that had been produced at the churches of St Thomas and St Nikolai, now entrusted to his care, comprised the modest attempts of his predecessor, Kuhnau. The importance of the enthusiasm and musical understanding of the people of Leipzig should never be underestimated, even if, understandably, they regarded the populist music of Telemann as more approachable than Bach's. However, the comment made in 1728 by the Leipzig poet and literary reformer, Johann Christoph Gottsched, praising Telemann, Handel and Bach as the three stars in the musical firmament,[72] shows that ears were not closed in Leipzig to Bach's more challenging writing.

Such broad recognition would hardly have been Bach's as a court Kapellmeister. Since he had still published very little, and probably only a few of his works circulated widely in manuscript copies, he needed the oxygen of an intellectually lively city, interested in art and science. The nobility

Johann Christoph Gottsched (1700–66) came to Leipzig one year after Bach, first as a teacher of poetry and later of logic and metaphysics. He campaigned for a higher level of German literature, on par with great English and French works. His *Moralische Wochenzeitschriften* was the most important literary magazine of his generation.

may have appreciated art, but they wanted to collect and enjoy it, rather than discuss it. Unsurprisingly, the rulers were unwilling to release the artists they esteemed from their service. The cultured and educated middle classes were becoming *defined* by their interest in art and science, discovering a particular identity through the discussion of science, philosophy and aesthetics. Bach, the quintessential deep-thinking artist, was surely eager to leave the intellectually straitened atmosphere of a court and breathe free city air. Particularly in his later years in Leipzig, he contributed to the public discussion of art in composition and literature, although at first, his creative work was mainly confined to the narrower field of sacred music.

Bach's move to Leipzig was reported by Hamburg's *Staats- und Gelehrten Zeitung*, on 4 June 1723: 'Last Saturday at noon, four carts loaded with household goods arrived here from Köthen, belonging to the former princely Kapellmeister there, who is appointed to Leipzig as Cantori Figurali. At two o'clock he arrived himself with his family, in two carriages, and moved into his newly renovated lodgings in the school of St Thomas's.'[73]

The renovation had cost over 100 thalers. Bach and his family moved into lodgings within the old walls of St Thomas's school (demolished at the beginning of the 20th century), right next door to St Thomas's church itself. After another rebuilding, in 1732 at the latest, Bach took over three floors of a whole wing of the building. An old photograph shows a modest room with a single window which, normally, was the study where he composed. His ceremonial induction into office took place on 1 June, and on this occasion Bach received permission to transfer his Latin lessons to the third master of the school in return for appropriate payment. Two days earlier he had

Johann Christian Bach (1735–82) came to London in 1762 as opera composer at the King's Theatre and soon acquired various royal appointments. From 1764, he promoted (with Karl Friedrich Abel) a series of subscription concerts which for the next two decades were the centre of London's musical life.

The brilliant, eldest son: Wilhelm Friedemann (1710–84). Painting, probably by W Weitsch, c.1760

The most famous son: Carl Philipp Emanuel (1714–88). Pastel by Johann Philipp Bach, c.1780

performed his inaugural music 'with great success', according to the press:[74] the work was the cantata BWV 75 for the first Sunday after Trinity, *Die Elenden sollen essen* (*The poor shall eat*).

Providing the people of Leipzig with such 'figural music' was to be Bach's main duty for his remaining 27 years. He had the resources of the 'first' and very capable choir of St Thomas's school available for its performance, and an instrumental ensemble of town musicians, supplemented by some of the older school pupils and by students. The liturgical setting was that of the 'early service with sermon', which began at seven o'clock and sometimes went on until eleven o'clock. The 'principal music' alternated weekly between St Thomas and St Nikolai. On many church festivals it had to be repeated at the 'evening service with sermon', beginning at quarter past one, in whichever church had not had 'music-making' earlier that morning.[75]

Family life must have been a lively affair in the relatively spacious Kantor's lodgings, even if the paterfamilias had many professional demands for his time. The children of his first marriage had increasing educational needs, and those of his second marriage were

The keyboard virtuoso: Johann Christoph Friedrich (1732–95), the 'Bückeburg Bach'. Pastel by Georg David Matthieu, *c.*1775

The cosmopolitan son: Johann Christian (1735–82), the 'London Bach'. Painting by Thomas Gainsborough

FAMILY LIFE

growing up fast. In June 1723, Wilhelm Friedemann and Carl Philipp Emanuel were accepted into St Thomas's school. At the end of that year, Bach put down the name of his eldest son, then aged 13, for the university, where he enrolled in 1729. Between 1723 and 1742, Anna Magdalena bore Bach 13 children, one a year until 1729; seven of them died soon after birth or in early childhood (not an unusually high mortality rate for the time). Of the three surviving daughters, Elisabeth Juliana married Bach's pupil Johann Christoph Altnickol. Two of the surviving sons became famous musicians: Johann Christoph Friedrich, born in 1732, the 'Bückeburg Bach'; and Johann Christian, three years younger, the 'London Bach'.

In 1725, Bach presented his wife with the *Notenbüchlein* bound in green, inscribed 'AMB' on the front in gold leaf and India ink. The music that was transcribed into this book over the next 15 years included vocal and keyboard pieces not only by Johann Sebastian, but Anna Magdalena herself, and children, friends and musical colleagues, such as Johann Hasse, Christian Petzold and Francois Couperin. This book is an invaluable record of the Bach family's music making and education. Bach wrote they were *all born musicians, and I can already form both vocal and instrumental ensembles within my family, particularly since my present wife sings in a good clear soprano, and my eldest daughter, too, joins in not badly.*[76]

The children had to be taught music. Here, Anna Magdalena was able to help. After all, she had been an acclaimed singer in Köthen. Now her main task was the onerous job of music copying, which was often needed in a hurry; even the first clumsy and then increasingly accomplished copying of the elder sons appears in the extant performance material. In spite of all this, there was still time for domestic music-making. In 1725, Bach prepared a second little book for his wife, beginning with two demanding works, the keyboard partitas BWV 827 in A minor and BWV 830 in E minor, but also containing songs and smaller pieces, most of them copied out by Anna Magdalena herself and her sons.

As Kantor of St Thomas's, Bach was an important figure. Pupils went in and out of his home, musicians asked him for references, town councils were anxious to have his expert advice on the organs in their churches and on making appointments to vacant positions. His everyday workload was heavy: examining new pupils, appointing town musicians and supervising the city's stocks of instruments. His arguments with the authorities about the rights and duties of the Kantor of St Thomas's may have further sapped his strength. In 1725, there was a dispute over which part Bach should take in the music of the university church, and how he was to be paid for it. One of the letters of complaint he wrote to the Elector on this subject runs to 16 closely-written pages. In 1728, the consistory told him that he could not prevent Pastor Gottlieb Gaudlitz from choosing the hymns for divine service, a right that Bach normally reserved for himself.

These arguments came to a climax in 1730. The choice of the new headmaster for St Thomas's school led to complaints about the Kantor, who did not ensure that the Latin teaching incumbent upon him was being capably given, did not give singing lessons, went away without asking leave, and so on. The members of the council who had always wanted a Kantor rather than a Music Director proposed a reduction in Bach's salary, on the grounds that he was 'incorrigible . . . A break would have to come some time'.[77] Bach replied the same month, in fact by return of post, with a letter running to ten pages and couched in anything but humble terms: *A Short but Most Necessary Draft for a Well-Appointed Church Music; With Certain Modest Reflections on the Decline of the Same.*

In this memorandum, Bach reproaches the council in detail for the inadequacy of his working conditions. Not all of the 16 singers at his disposal are sufficiently qualified. Of the 20 instrumentalists who would be required to assure musical taste and present new kinds of music, he has only eight available, and they are semi-retired town musicians. *Modesty*, says Bach, *forbids me to speak at all truthfully of their qualities and musical knowledge*. The activities of students and school pupils who have helped him out before have been restricted by the withdrawal of fees or stipends – *for who will do work or perform services for nothing?*[78]

Bach suggests to those of the city fathers who are ignorant of art that *the state of music is quite different from what it was, since our artistry has increased very much, and the gusto has changed astonishingly, and accordingly the former style of music no longer seems to please our ears.* Although he was an official pledged to subordination, Bach could hardly have put it more clearly: instead of reproaching the Kantor for neglecting his duties, the council ought to provide its 'director musices' with better working conditions so that he could give the city up-to-date instrumental music that would attract attention. The whole thing sounds almost like an angry farewell to Leipzig, and in fact two months later Bach enumerated the points of what he felt was an unendurable situation in a letter to his childhood friend Erdmann, who was the Russian envoy to Danzig:

But since (1) I find that the post is by no means so lucrative as it had been described to me; (2) I have failed to obtain many of the fees pertaining to the office; (3) the place is very expensive; and (4) the authorities are odd and little interested in music, so that I must live amid almost continual vexation, envy, and persecution; accordingly I shall be forced, with God's help, to seek my fortune elsewhere. Should Your Honour know or find a suitable post in your city for an old and faithful servant, I beg you most humbly to put in a most gracious word of recommendation for me – I shall not fail to do my best to give satisfaction and justify your most gracious intercession on my behalf. My present post amounts to about 700 thaler, and when there are rather more funerals than usual, the fees rise in proportion; but when a healthy wind blows, they fall accordingly, as for example last year, when I lost fees that would ordinarily come in from funerals to an amount of more than 100 thaler. In Thuringia I could get along better on 400 thaler than here with twice that many, because of the excessively high cost of living.[79]

Even in his earlier Leipzig period, Bach did not rely on being appreciated by the authorities, *odd and little interested in music* as they were. His regular return visits to Köthen, sometimes bringing Anna

Magdalena as a singer, suggest how important it must have been for him to be able to continue to call himself a court Kapellmeister. Two years after the first performance of the *St Matthew Passion* he appropriated ten movements from it for the funeral cantata for Prince Leopold, *Klagt Kinder, klagt es aller Welt* (*Lament, children, lament to all the world*) BWV 244a, a very unusual thing to do, for while the funeral cantata was of a sacred nature it was none the less written for a human being. Perhaps Bach felt so unappreciated in Leipzig, even for a mighty work like the *St Matthew Passion*, that he wanted to offer it in a new context to a more sensitive public.

The academic audience for whom Bach composed congratulatory addresses on literary texts in 1725 and 1726 would have been knowledgeable and enthusiastic too. These were cantatas BWV 205, 249a and 207, including *Der zufriedengestellte Äolus* (*Aeolus satisfied*), a tribute to the university professor August Friedrich Müller. Bach was not offering his Leipzig public casually composed occasional works, but pieces conceived on a grand scale and written using expansive tone-painting, a style which he appropriately called *dramma per musica*. Gottsched's definition of this description was that it covered 'little operas or operettas' which, however, 'are seldom seen on stage, but only for the most part sung in rooms'. In the same genre are many congratulatory or funeral works that Bach wrote for his Saxon sovereign in Dresden, a place to which he obviously felt powerfully attracted. However, church music, despite all his other activities, formed the undisputed centre of his early work in Leipzig.

Bach's first work for the church of St Nikolai, *Die Elenden sollen essen*, was the beginning of a major undertaking. Within a few years, he was working on five cycles of annual cantatas (this is the number given in the *Obituary*). That is, sequences of 60 cantatas for all the Sundays and holy days of the church year. The Kantor of St Thomas's could, of course, be expected to bring with him a good supply of Sunday cantatas, or to write new ones, since thinking in terms of

CANTATA SEQUENCES

self-contained annual cantata cycles was very much the rule at the time. But Bach set to work with remarkable enthusiasm. For years he not only rehearsed and performed a cantata relating to the time of the church year, week after week, but nearly always composed a new one, or for the major festivals sometimes three. He relieved his burden by reviving works composed in Weimar and Köthen, converting secular cantatas to sacred cantatas (in the 'parody' tradition). Sometimes he resorted to playing pieces by his cousin Johann Ludwig of Meiningen.

Reconstructing the details from the manuscript sources still entails problems. The manuscripts of Bach's works were scattered after his death, and a considerable number of sources have been lost entirely. To determine the order and dates of the cantatas that have come down to us piecemeal, not complete in their cycles, scholars have turned to the origin of the paper used or identified the handwriting of the various copyists. Identifying watermarks provide rough classification: one kind of paper indicates Weimar, a second Köthen, a third Bach's early Leipzig period, and so on.

The study of handwriting is helpful for more exact dating. Bach's own notation changed noticeably over the years – for instance, in his shaping of clefs, key signatures, the heads and tails of the notes, and in the general effect. There are equally important clues in the handwriting of his Leipzig copyists, who included family members and selected pupils of St Thomas's: once the anonymous clerks are identified from other documents, their work for Bach can be assigned comparatively well to a particular period. (A few years ago, three books of texts from Bach's early Leipzig period came to light, and confirmed the reliability of the hypothetical calendar of performance that had been drawn up in this way in certain important respects.)[80]

The first cycle of Leipzig cantatas, *Die Elenden sollen essen*, established Bach's 'programme' within the genre. The form he preferred is not unusual, and is often described as the 'mixed madrigal cantata'. 'Madrigal' means that its central section consists of a sequence of recitatives and arias to original texts. 'Mixed' denotes that this usually solo central section is flanked by two important outer movements: a 'concerto' almost always performed by the chorus on a Biblical text or a hymn forms the opening movement; and the closing movement is usually a straightforward hymn-setting.

This large-scale form was initially understood as a compromise between 'sacred' and 'art' music. The church wanted a musical expression of the symbols of faith, the Biblical text and the chorale, while the art of the Enlightenment, mainly originating in courts, saw no difference between a sacred and a secular cantata, and certainly no formal difference between the secular cantata and the opera.

For Bach, the great theological and artistic challenge of sacred music grew out of these dynamics, which a Leipzig Kantor (unlike, perhaps, a Weimar *Konzertmeister*) had to respect as a given. He himself was enough of a theologian to feel passionate enthusiasm for the Biblical texts and chorales at the centre of his sacred vocal music. But at the same time, he was an artist who felt equally passionate about the creative exploration of innovations in music, particularly those coming out of Italy.

Bach would have noted that on taking up his post he was warned not to compose in too theatrical or operatic a style, but the citizens of Leipzig were merely imposing on him, as a condition of service, something that had, after all, long been his higher purpose. Bach himself expressed social contradictions such as those between 'church' and 'art' with a cogency that often went far beyond the aesthetic horizons of his patrons. Even if it took centuries to prove his own aesthetic theories, for the time being Bach would have to endure the formal definitions forced upon him by these people, such as the 'correct' sacred style.

The 'mixed madrigal cantata', like the term itself, is formally and aesthetically an absurdity. Even so, this was the framework on which Bach constructed an impressive variety of approaches to the church cantata. The opening cantata, *Die Elenden sollen essen* is a useful model to analyse this form. The idea probably came to Bach in Köthen, and it has features which any Kapellmeister might compose. Despite those generic idioms it serves as well as any other cantata. In all, about 200 cantatas survive, composed or revived by Bach in Leipzig. According to the *Obituary* there must once have been about 300.

The text of the opening music is a paraphrase of the readings for the second Sunday after Whit Sunday: the parable of the rich man and the impoverished Lazarus (Luke 16: 19–31), and the Epistle on the love of God. The words begin with a suitable verse of a psalm, which is followed by the 'madrigal' text with the usual recitative and aria pattern. While the statements made in the Gospel and Epistle are explained in the recitatives as if in a sermon, and are applied *ad hominem*, that is to say to individuals, the Christian who is thus addressed expresses his love of the Saviour in the first person: *Mein Herze gläubt und liebt. Denn Jesu süsse Flammen, aus den' die meinen stammen, gehn über mich zusammen, weil er sich mir ergibt.* (*My heart believes and loves. For the sweet flames of Jesus, from which my own arise, envelop me within them, for he gives himself to me.*) A verse of the hymn *Was Gott tut, das ist wohlgetan* (*What God does is well done*) is sung as the close of the first half of the cantata, which was performed before the sermon, and another at the very end as the traditional concluding chorale.

Such a text reflects subtly the conditions in Leipzig: the Biblical text and chorale standing for *traditional* faith; the interpretation to be found in the recitatives is a *rational* one; the devotion to Jesus determining the tone of the arias is marked by a moderate kind of *Pietism*, which by now was accepted even by the dominant orthodoxy of Leipzig. The name of the librettist, who obviously had some theological training, is unknown, as is true of most of the other cantatas of that first year. Clearly, Bach was always on the lookout for suitable texts. Not until the third year did he use texts by such well-known Leipzig poets as Christian Friedrich Henrici, known as Picander, and Marianne von Ziegler, daughter of the former Mayor

Romanus; but it is likely that the author of the texts for the second year of chorale cantatas was from Leipzig and probably a clergyman.

Bach begins the cantata with an instrumental movement of elegiac splendour, imitating the course of the French overture, above which he wrote the word *Concerto*. The free polyphonic chorus *Die Elenden . . .* is built into it, so that the two independent structures interlock without losing their individual strengths. The first section, which might be called a prelude, is followed by a fugue performed by the chorus with instrumental accompaniment. The traditional motet genre underlies this second section, although Bach gives it new features: the singing voices are more strongly 'instrumentalised' in their extended melismatic parts than anything yet heard in Leipzig. At the same time, the melody explains the content of the text. The sad fate of the starving poor is expressed with as much force as the peace of eternity and the vicissitudes of life.

The instrumental *Sinfonia*, which introduces the second part of the cantata, sounds surprisingly like an excerpt from one of the *Brandenburg Concerti*. This immediately takes an even more surprising turn: the full orchestral sound is penetrated by a trumpet in its highest register playing the chorale melody *Was Gott tut, das ist wohlgetan* with which the first part of the cantata ended. Thus, Bach sublimely unites the secular and sacred, the autonomous and functional planes. Aesthetically, this is a bold venture, since musically the two planes are hardly counterpointed but harmonised with each other. The audience – the congregation – must unite what, in terms of sound alone, may still be disparate.

The recitatives, some of them accompanied by strings, are in an operatic parlando style, but characteristically of Bach are rich in gesture, strongly emotional and strikingly explicit. The deceptive superfluity of the rich man's wealth is depicted with as much care as the arch of Heaven or the descent to Hell. The diversity of structural devices that Bach offers in the four arias of the cantata begins with the instrumentation: the oboe d'amore was a new instrument

Bach's partner among the council musicians: Johann Gottfried Reiche. Without such virtuoso instrumentalists as the trumpeter Reiche, the senior musician among the Leipzig town pipers, Bach could not have performed his church and chamber music in Leipzig adequately. Painting by Elias Gottlob Haussmann, c.1725

at the time, and when using the high, C-sharp trumpet Bach was relying on the skill of Leipzig's famous virtuoso trumpeter Johann Gottfried Reiche. The treatment of the singing voices moves between the virtuosity of the soprano aria and the Pietistic simplicity of the tenor and alto arias. The models determining the course of the separate arias suggest the dance forms sarabande, polonaise, minuet and passepied; the forms constantly reflect specific expositions of the categories of concerto, ritornello and *da capo*, and of contrapuntal and thematic work.

Bach did not always allow magnificence and imagination such scope as in this opening piece. Some cantatas he might almost have composed in his sleep, and there are certain arias that seem to be running on automatic pilot. But, on the whole, the lack of purely 'routine' composition is astonishing.

In his second year at Leipzig (1724–5) Bach set himself a new and fundamental task: he composed a cycle of chorale cantatas for the year complete up to the time between Easter and Trinity, thus facing the question of how to take the vocal chorale arrangement, a genre with a rich tradition behind it in Leipzig but now antiquated, and combine it with something more modern.

Working on his third cycle, Bach allowed himself to go at a rather slower pace: he borrowed cantatas from the second year's cycle, and performed works by his cousin Johann Ludwig of Meiningen. Consequently, he took almost three years to construct the complete cycle. This is more varied in form than its predecessors, sometimes deviating from the rule that the opening movement of a cantata must be a setting of a Biblical or chorale text, and beginning instead with a solo setting of an original verse. Bach composed many cantata movements based on earlier instrumental works and/or organ solos. Clearly, he was losing interest in formally unified cantata cycles, or cycles written to a schematic pattern of the kind popular with his contemporaries. As a result, it is uncertain whether he finished the fourth cycle written for him by his librettist Picander in 1728–9. At the very least, only a few pieces survive, and these show a tendency to simpler structures.

Almost no trace of a fifth cycle survives, just a few pieces from Bach's later creative period, mainly filling in gaps in the earlier cycles.[81] Presumably, having worked to his own satisfaction on the 'church cantata', Bach was ever more inclined to draw on his own earlier works or those of other composers. As so few contemporary sources mention either his retreat from the genre so central to his official work or the overflowing productivity of the early Leipzig years, it is clear that Bach received little public acclaim for this work. It is all the more understandable that he sought other fields of activity which would attract more attention.

Besides the composition and performance of the Sunday cantatas, Bach's duties included the writing of occasional works, such as cantatas for the inauguration of a new council or motets for other special occasions. The great motets using double choirs in the great central German Bach tradition were generally intended for funerals. Most of Bach's were probably written in the early Leipzig years. They include *Singet dem Herrn ein neues Lied* (*Sing unto the Lord a new song*), BWV 225; *Der Geist hilft unser Schwachheit auf* (*The Holy Spirit helps our weakness*), BWV 226; *Komm, Jesu, komm* (*Come, Jesus, come*), BWV 229; and *Fürchte dich nicht, ich bin bei dir* (*Fear not, for I am with thee*), BWV 228. The chorale motet *Jesu, meine Freude* (*Jesus, my delight*), BWV 227, occupies a special position. This is a work with a complicated compositional history, with a sequence of closing movements arranged in skilful symmetry, breaking the mould of sacred music written for a functional purpose.

The same complexity is true of two works setting Latin texts: the *Magnificat* BWV 243a, performed at Christmas 1723, with inserted German passages in the nature of folk-song such as *Freut euch und jubiliert* (*Be glad and rejoice*), and the *Sanctus* performed at Christmas the following year, the earliest part of what would become the *B-minor Mass*.

Above all, however, it applies to the two most important works resulting from Bach's early Leipzig period: the *St John Passion* and the *St Matthew Passion*. Both works arose from Bach's duties in his office as Kantor, but also reflect his wish to free his sacred music from too close a connection with the liturgy and make it, as Georg Philipp Telemann called one of his cantata cycles, a 'harmonious divine service' in itself. The two *Passions* were both performed in the course of a church service with a sermon, Vespers on Good Friday. But that service tended to be merely the occasion for an institution long known in Hamburg, the sacred concert which might even be performed in places other than churches.

To a certain extent, Bach planned the performance of his first

The original place of performance for the *St John Passion*: the church of St Nikolai, Leipzig, *c.*1785. Watercolour by Carl Benjamin Schwarz

Leipzig *Passion* on Good Friday 1724 on his own initiative. He had the text of the 'musical arias' printed and distributed in advance – an unusual procedure in Leipzig – to advertise its performance, and to earn a little money from the sales. On his own authority, he named St Thomas's church as the place of performance on the title page. Perhaps he was unaware of a decision by the council that it was the turn of St Nikolai that year, but probably mainly because performance conditions were better there.

He was summoned to the city hall and told to have a correction printed at the council's expense. In this he explained what had happened to his 'respected auditors' so self-confidently that the superintendent issued a formal reprimand instructing him 'to take more care in future'.[82] Changes in the second version, performed the following year, may be explained by the necessity of respecting the views of the Leipzig authorities after they had looked at the work very closely. Perhaps they complained of its poetic freedom and musical emotion; in short, of excessive theatricality.

The *Passion According to St John* was followed in 1727 by the *St Matthew Passion*, and by a lost *St Mark Passion* in 1731. A *St Luke Passion*, BWV 246, performed in 1730, is now believed to be a joint work by the Bach family using earlier compositions by Johann Sebastian. Bach probably performed a *Passion* every year in Leipzig, reviving and revising his own works in addition to presenting those of other composers including Reinhard Keiser, Georg Philipp Telemann, George Frideric Handel and Karl Heinrich Graun.

In his two great *Passions*, Bach followed the formal and stylistic path on which he had already set out in his church cantatas. The libretti are based on the Biblical Passion story, adding suitable hymns and madrigal-like texts that Bach could set as recitatives, ariosi, arias and choruses. In the case of the *St John Passion*, it was based on a famous Passion text by Barthold Heinrich Brockes, and in the case of the *St Matthew Passion* it was written specially by his Leipzig librettist Picander. The dimensions assumed by both works were excitingly new. What other contemporaneous musical genre of any kind could offer movements on such a grand scale as the opening choruses *Herr, unser Herrscher* (*Lord, our ruler*) and *Kommt, ihr Töchter, helft mir klagen* (*Come, ye daughters, help my mourning*)? From the start, Bach makes it clear that he will not be content to write the kind of work that tended to restrict itself to a series of single numbers similar to the Baroque opera. Regardless of the guidelines laid down by the sacrosanct Passion story, these were to be coherent structures, as mighty as they were richly organised, monuments for posterity.

Above all, the *St Matthew Passion* may be the first instance of a composer presenting a single comprehensive work as an aesthetic entity *sui generis*, with the unity of a work of architecture. Bach's wish to create music with relevance outside its sacred and social functions is evident in that the last version of the *St Matthew Passion* has been preserved in perhaps the cleanest score he ever wrote; he entered the words of the Evangelist and the chorale *O Lamm Gottes unschuldig* (*O innocent Lamb of God*) in red ink, and later, in the stiff script of his old age, carefully tried to repair a place where the manuscript had been damaged. To link the *St Matthew Passion* with later ideas of the autonomous work of art does not, of course, mean overlooking its original function, or seeing its general and particular structure as a puzzle by speculating on numerical meanings. Bach's *Passions* were written for the daily round of Leipzig. The mere fact that details were altered for every revival should warn us against too much arithmetical speculation over the symbolic meaning of certain numbers of notes and bars.

Even if such inquiry turned out to some extent to be justified, it cannot replace appreciation of the aesthetic value of the works, which is evident on other levels: in the symphonic weight of the opening movements, the almost realistic drama of many of the choruses (*Kreuzige! – Crucify!*), the stylistic richness of the evangelist's passages, and the exquisite ariosi and arias, which mingle the presentation of intense emotion with graphic cogency and deeply felt symbolism. It is almost incredible that, after the cantatas, Bach could go even further, producing musical gem after gem. The year when he wrote the *St Matthew Passion* he was 41, in his artistic prime. Later, he composed works of a similar quality to the two *Passions*, and even more masterly. But the magnificent combination of strong emotion and reflection, drama and spirituality, remained unsurpassed.

The composer and theorist Carl Friedrich Zelter (1758–1832) was a student of Fasch and his first noted work was a funeral cantata on the death of Frederick the Great in 1786. In 1800, he became the conductor of the Berlin *Singverein* and went on to found the *Ripienschule* to encourage good orchestral practise, and later the *Liedertafel*. His students included, amongst others, Mendelssohn, Loewe and Meyerbeer. His advocacy of Bach's music inspired Mendelssohn and Devrient to revive the *Matthew Passion* in 1829.

For a long time after Bach's death, the *St Matthew Passion* was merely a subject for private study by connoisseurs and music lovers. Carl Friedrich Zelter (1758–1832) performed parts of it at the Berliner Singakademie in the early 19th century, partly out of genuine admiration for the work, partly in line with an Enlightenment view of music which condescendingly thought it necessary to remove the surface 'froth' of the period before the 'bright light' of the content of the music might shine through. It was left to Felix Mendelssohn-Bartholdy, at the age of just 20, to rekindle the true spirit of the *St Matthew Passion* in 1829, with the keen eye of a musical kindred soul. He revived it in a way that, very much in the Romantic spirit, allowed hearers to guess at those elements of the work that transcend time and make it aesthetically impossible to fit it into the temporally linked history of style. Goethe wrote: 'Your latest [letter], with news of the happy performance of that great musical work of the past, gives me food for thought. It is as if I heard the sea breaking in the distance. I send you congratulations on the perfect success of what can hardly be represented.'[83]

The 'court composer':
Bach's middle Leipzig period
FROM 1729

The people of Leipzig had not only the *Leipziger Kirchen-Staat* to guide them through the 22 weekly church services with sermons, and the countless shorter prayer services held in a city whose inhabitants were counted 'fortunate' for that reason,[84] but also *Das jetzt lebende und jetzt florirende Leipzig* (*Leipzig Living and Flourishing Today*), a guide to secular life. The 1732 edition reads: 'There are two regular *Collegia Musica*: 1) meets under the direction of Herr Kantor Bach at Herr Gottfried Zimmermann's, on Wednesdays in the garden from four to six o'clock in summer time, and on Fridays in the coffee house in Catharinen-Strasse in the evening from eight till ten o'clock in the winter; 2) meets on Thursdays from eight till ten o'clock under the direction of Herr Johann Gottl. Görner, organist at St Thomas's church, in the Schell-hafer house on Kloster-Gasse.'[85]

The Leipzig setting in which Bach the 'secular' musician worked: Zimmermann's coffee house at 14 Catharinen-Strasse, destroyed in the Second World War. This is where Bach performed his *Coffee Cantata* as well as many of his concerti and chamber compositions. Engraving after Johann Georg Schreiber

In 1729, Back took over the direction of the *Collegium Musicum* in Zimmermann's coffee house. This marked a watershed in Bach's life; he had completed his planned annual cantata cycles and was ready for something new. He succeeded his friend Georg Balthasar

Schott, who until now had been organist of the *Neukirche*. Presumably Schott's successor as organist, Carl Gotthelf Gerlach, would also have had the right to direct the *Collegium Musicum*, but Gerlach was Bach's pupil and probably glad to have been recommended by him for the *Neukirche* appointment.

Bach continued to be Kantor of St Thomas's, but that next year he entered into bitter controversy with the authorities, who accused him of neglecting his duty. He countered that they took no interest in art. Clearly, he no longer wished to be a Kantor bound by the hierarchy of the system, but longed for the freedom of an artist legitimately operating in a wider field. His frustration was apparent even before 1729, but became increasingly so thereafter.

This change of direction is most clearly illustrated by Bach's attempts to obtain honorary or even real offices in foreign courts. His honorary title of Kapellmeister of Köthen had formally lapsed in 1728, after the death of Prince Leopold. Bach seems to have acquired a similar position at the court of Weissenfels around that time. Also, he energetically pursued success at the presitigious electoral court in Dresden. From 1727 onwards, he busily composed much birthday, name-day, coronation, wedding and funeral music for the Elector of Saxony and King of Poland, the Electress and the Electoral Princes. These were minor pieces but taken as a whole represent a large well of creative activity. Today this attracts little attention only because the pious texts no longer have any functional relevance. Bach, as if he had foreseen their future obsolescence, re-used most of them in sacred works, particularly the *Christmas Oratorio*.

Bach used the *Collegium Musicum* for the homage cantatas, the one institution in Leipzig allowed to give performances of such works. Since the town musicians were a closed corporation, they could perform only in the service of the city. The city council would have hardly wished to pay homage to the electoral house, a regular civic institution equivalent to the annual celebrations for the inauguration of the new council. The business of the university

The desirable alternative: Dresden. Bach wanted few things as much as the title of court composer. The cosmopolitan nature of Dresden would make him forget the constraints and subservience that he had to bear in Leipzig.
The Neumarkt, Dresden. Painting by Canaletto (Bernardo Bellotto), 1753

was to promote such music, and Bach acted as an official musical intermediary between Leipzig and Dresden in the university's service. When the elector or his envoys came to Leipzig to receive congratulations of various kinds, Bach met them as *Spiritus Rector*. An account, published in 1773, by Johann Adolph Scheibe, a contemporary who was extremely critical of Bach, said that, 'detailed and reliable news could be obtained almost daily' of musical life in Dresden, since Bach and other musical figures of Leipzig were in regular contact 'with the virtuosos of the royal Kapelle'.[86]

Therefore, it was by no means a spontaneous gesture when Bach dedicated the *Kyrie* and *Gloria* of the later *B-minor Mass* to Friedrich August on his accession in July 1733. He presented it as a self-contained work, as the *Missa Brevis*. In the accompanying document he expressly petitioned the Catholic Elector for a *title with His Highness's Court Kapelle*, perhaps

While the Principality of Saxony was Lutheran, the prince – who was also the King of Poland – was Catholic. So it is not surprising that Bach dedicated a Latin mass to the King, with portions that could be performed in Lutheran church services as well.

putting himself into contention for the post of court Kapellmeister. This had been vacant for some time and was still not officially filled.

The *Missa Brevis* was performed in Dresden[86] but did not immediately bring the swift advancement Bach might have expected. So he composed more *ommagi* and made sure that news of these appeared in the Leipzig press. In the autumn of 1736, another petition to the elector finally had the desired effect: on 19 November Bach received the appointment as 'Composer to the court Kapelle'. Scarcely two weeks later he was in Dresden expressing his gratitude by giving recitals on the new organ in the church of Our Lady, thus adding to his exalted reputation.[88]

No doubt he also wanted the appointment because complaints about his neglect of the office of Kantor were accumulating, and Bach was constantly having to seek justification from his sovereign. The 'dispute of the prefects', in which Bach argued for his right to appoint his choral prefects (assistants) himself, took place just before he was appointed composer to the court. In his subsequent quarrel with the authorities, which went on for years, it was useful to him that although the court in Dresden merely sent his complaints on to the Leipzig Consistory, it always termed him 'our Court Composer'. He was not, he may have thought, delivered up entirely defenceless to the Leipzig authorities.

Although the records are very forthcoming about the dispute as to whether or not the Rektor could go against the Kantor's will in substituting an unmusical prefect for an unruly one, they say nothing about the eventual outcome. Nor do the sources show any reasons why, once Bach had been appointed court composer, he reduced considerably his activities on behalf of the electoral house of Saxony, although he had formerly *most obediently offered to show my untiring industry whenever your Royal Highness should graciously require the composition of either sacred or orchestral music*. The services he had offered were not required, and he became increasingly interested in other tasks.

COURT COMPOSER

Previously, writing music for the court in Dresden had certainly been an attractive proposition – Bach was largely his own master in this field, negotiating with librettists, getting books of his texts printed on his own account, drawing fees from the university and, presumably, receiving presents from the nobility to whom he paid tribute in his music. Undoubtedly, he enjoyed working with enthusiastic students and the best town musicians more than making music with the usual church ensemble. Thus, Bach also came into contact with the 'educated' and 'elegant' society of Leipzig, such as Gottsched, who in 1727 wrote the text for the *Tombeau* BWV 198 on the death of Electress Christiane Eberhardine; it opens with the line *Lass, Fürstin, lass noch einen Strahl* (*Allow, Princess, but one more ray*).

In the 17th century, the *Tombeau* was an instrumental piece composed as a memorial for high-standing individuals and artists. The English *Tears*, the French *Plainte* and the Italian *Lamento* belonged to the same tradition. Some vocal pieces were also called *Tombeau*, but not until the 18th century.

It is doubtful whether such texts meant more to Bach than the sacred verses he more usually set, which were also very much of their time in their choice of words and images. However, one can imagine the satisfaction he derived from pursuing such activities independently of the powerful ecclesiastic and civic hierarchies. In this context his close relationship with Picander, who wrote the libretti not only for the *St Matthew Passion* but for most of Bach's festival and congratulatory cantatas, speaks volumes.

Under his real name of Christian Friedrich Henrici, Picander had worked his way up to being collector of the local land and municipal liquor taxes. As a young student, firmly determined to make his way as a writer, he enjoyed early success in Leipzig with risqué wedding verses. In all, he said, he wrote 436 such *carmina*, 'often in night and fog . . . when not the faintest poetic star shone down upon me.'[89] Later he became a writer of comic dramas, such as *Der Academische Schlendrian* (*The Academic Slacker*), *Der Ertzt-Säuffer* (*The Arch-Drunkard*) and *Die Weiber-Probe* (*The Test of Women*). These described sections of Leipzig society so clearly that the city council banned them outright.

Why was Bach on such a familiar footing with a man who was apparently a wastrel? At least it is remarkable that they both had increasing success with their congratulatory cantatas. Bach's name now featured frequently in the press, although not in such lengthy articles as the account by the city chronicler Johann Salomon Riemer, who reported on 5 October 1734 on the performance of cantata BWV 215, *Preise dein Glücke, gesegnetes Sachsen* (*Praise thy good fortune, blessed Saxony*): 'At nine o'clock in the evening the students of the university here offered a fine evening serenade with many wax tapers, and, to the sound of trumpets and drums, in front of the Apel house on the marketplace, a most humble drama, which had been composed and was performed by the Kapellmeister, Mr. Joh. Sebastian Bach. Six hundred students carried wax candles, and four counts [from among the students] acted as marshals to present the music. The procession made its way along Ritterstrasse, Brühlstrasse and Catherinen-Strasse to the king's lodging, and when the musicians had reached the weighhouse the trumpeters and drummers went up on it, and some went from the Rathaus to form a choir. When the text was presented, the four counts were permitted to kiss hands, and his Royal Majesty with her Royal Highness his wife and the Royal Princes did not leave the window as long as the music played, but most graciously listened to it, and it pleased their Majesties greatly.'[90]

Seven hundred copies of the text were printed, and Bach received a fee of 50 thalers, almost a month's salary. No less important was the social status he achieved by presenting such pieces with the *Collegium Musicum*, which did not perform only on festive occasions but attracted attention through its weekly rehearsals. Lorenz Christoph Mizler, in his *Musikalische Bibliothek* published in Leipzig in 1736, referred to the rehearsals of the *Collegia Musica* 'musical concerts': 'The members who give these musical concerts consist for the most part of the gentlemen who are students here, and there are always good musicians among them, so that in time, as is well known, they frequently become famous virtuosi. Every musician may be heard in public at these musical concerts, and for the most part the audience are such as can judge the value of each skilful musician.'[91]

Bach's activities were more than an attempt to win honours and offices at court, and were the quintessence of that kind of middle-class music-making in which experts and amateurs alike were represented among both performers and audience, conducting musical discourse in what we may assume was the relaxed atmosphere of a rehearsal, something that the rigid rituals of the later symphony concert hardly permitted. From 1729 to the early 1740s, with only a two-year interruption, Bach provided his *Collegium Musicum* with new music every week, fulfilling a quota of work which may not quite have equalled his exertions in figural music for Sundays and church festivals, but was considerable enough to explain his gradual dropping of cantata composition.

The achievements of Bach and Johann Gottlieb Görner – who seems to have worked with the senior Kantor of St Thomas's in this field – in their respective *Collegia Musica* in Leipzig prepared the ground for the founding in 1743 of 'Great' or 'Merchants' Concerts, a separate entity from the *Collegia Musica*. While not the first such institution, this was the most important forerunner of the Leipzig Gewandhaus concerts, the supreme embodiment of this specifically middle-class cultural entity.[92]

Bach's contact with the court musicians of Dresden suggests that he did not confine himself to performances of his own works in his *Collegium*, but was receptive to many kinds of new music. Many of the musical manuscripts to be found in Leipzig today belonged to his *Collegium Musicum*: these include Italian cantatas by George Frideric Handel and Niccoló Antonio Porpora, and instrumental music by Antonio Vivaldi, Pietro Locatelli and Tommaso Albinoni.[93]

With the exception of the *Brandenburg Concerti*, most of the orchestral works hitherto claimed for the Köthen period exist only in manuscripts of the Leipzig period. It is possible that much of the music attributed to the 'Köthen' Kapellmeister (perhaps including the sonatas with obbligato harpsichord accompaniment) were not written until the composer came to Leipzig. Even if Bach had to leave all his orchestral material behind for the use of the Kapelle, this does not explain why there are extant sketches for Köthen 'originals'. Therefore, it is unlikely that the 'overture' in B minor BWV 1067, which has come down to us only in a set of parts from 1738–9, dates from Köthen. Its final version with obbligato flute may well have been a farewell present to Carl Philipp Emanuel, who was appointed harpsichordist to Crown Prince Friedrich of Prussia, later King Friedrich II (Frederick the Great) in 1738.

Frederick the Great was once playing a flute concerto by his court flautist and teacher Quantz, whilst Carl Philipp Emanuel Bach, playing continuo on the fortepiano, directed the performance. At one point, Quantz unexpectedly entered the room, unsettling his royal student, who became nervous and missed an entry. Bach immediately covered the mistake, providing a florid keyboard roulade. After the performance, the King insisted that the mistake be made moot, and that Quantz should write Carl Philip Emanuel's face-saving figuration into the text.

An argument against the dating of many concerti to the Leipzig period is that Bach transcribed many of them along with solo concerti by Vivaldi and other composers for one or more solo harpsichords. There seems no reason why he should have composed concerti for melodic instruments in Leipzig, only to rearrange them *immediately* as harpsichord concerti.

Clearly, Bach favoured the harpsichord as a concerto instrument during his time with the *Collegium Musicum*. Initially, he was concerned to give his two eldest sons concert experience before they left home, Wilhelm Friedemann to his appointment as organist of St Sophia's in Dresden in 1733, Carl Philipp Emanuel a year later to continue his studies in Frankfurt an der Oder. In 1735, Bach said approvingly of his pupil Ludwig Krebs, that *he need not be afraid to be heard*,[94] an attitude that he will have also encouraged in his sons. All the concerti for two to four harpsichords BWV 1060–1065 were written for this purpose: the harpsichord concerto in D minor, BWV 1052a, may have been revised in 1734 by C P E Bach himself for his own use. Most of these pieces are recognisable rearrangements of other works; the concerto for four harpsichords derives from Antonio Vivaldi's *Concerto Grosso* Op 3 No 10, from the *L'estro armonico*.

It must have been extraordinary when Bach arranged a concert for four violins of Antonio Vivaldi's Op 3, No 10 in his Leipzig *Collegium Musicum*, using an unprecedented four harpsichords for the première. If even single-harpsichord concerts were a novelty, events with four keyboard instruments must have been a sensation.

Thus, while Bach perhaps introduced his sons to opportunities offered by the concerto, he probably presented himself as a soloist with the seven transcriptions of his own concerti BWV 1052–1058. These are contained in a collected volume made by Bach himself around 1740, and include keyboard versions of the two famous violin concerti (BWV 1041, 1042) and the fourth *Brandenburg Concerto*. Perhaps created in knowledge of the organ concerti of George Frideric Handel, which had appeared in 1738,[95] these serve as a valuable record of Bach's own performance style. After all, he was very familiar with them, and famously extemporised on them.[96]

There is a huge debate today about the composition date of Bach's solo concerts and orchestra overtures, as revealed in the controversy surrounding the B minor suite for the flute and orchestra. It was formerly believed that Bach wrote it while in Köthen. This estimate was later revised to 1738–9 because the only existing manuscript is from these years. But a violin version from the 1730s probably pre-dated the flute variation, so in recent publications Bach experts have again placed the piece in Köthen.

While tradition has it that the strict three-part sonatas for organ, BWV 525–530, were used as teaching works for Wilhelm Friedemann, similar works for other ensembles can be assigned to the Leipzig *Collegium Musicum*. These include the sonatas for flute

BWV 1030 and 1032, and for viola da gamba BWV 1027–1029.

The vocal music performed by Bach with his *Collegium Musicum* consisted largely of his own compositions. The texts of lively works about the evils of coffee-drinking (BWV 211), the virtues of cheerfulness (BWV 204) and the advantages of Leipzig, *the elect city on the Pleisse* (BWV 216a) reflect the tastes of the middle class, while the libretto for the *Dispute Between Phoebus and Pan* (BWV 201) reflects the concerns of Leipzig academia, that centre of literature and university scholarship. In making Apollo and Mercury debate whether Leipzig achieved fame and fortune by scholarship or trade, Bach may have been merely providing his dutiful eulogy to the city. However, when the *Coffee Cantata* aptly premièred at Zimmermann's coffee house, he was participating in a topic of the moment. Did coffee foster the cheerful spirit appropriate to a good citizen, or was it a dangerous temptation to which a modest person should not be exposed?

The *Peasant Cantata* BWV 212, composed in 1742, is a 'cabinet piece' of realistic or perhaps cryptically artful confrontation between the worlds of peasants, citizens and courtiers. Two middle-class citizens, Bach and Picander, unite their talents to pay tribute to von Dieskau, nobleman, tax overseer and district captain of Leipzig, on his inheritance of the small estate of Klein-Zschocher. At the same time, they wanted to describe in detail the wretched situation of the peasants under such rubrics as 'Poverty', 'Punishment' and 'Military Service', making not entirely innocuous jokes about the new master, in the 'frame' of a *cantata burlesque*. Presumably, von Dieskau had passed the text in advance. We do not know how far the performers were aware of their own respective roles in all of the cryptic symbolism of this parlour game. All we can say for sure is that the Bach of the *Peasant Cantata* was far from ignorant of worldly concerns.[97]

Besides his duties as Kantor and with the *Collegium Musicum*, and linked activities for the court of Dresden, in his middle Leipzig period Bach deliberately conquered the field of keyboard music with the four parts of the *Klavierübung*. His first steps were very cautious. On 1 November 1726, Bach announced in the *Leipziger-Post-Zeitungen* to *lovers of the keyboard* that he intended *to publish an opus of keyboard suites*, and had indeed *already made a start with the first partitas*.[98] Shortly before, the B major partita BWV 825 was engraved; this was the first imprint of his music for which he was personally responsible.

Bach chose the moniker *Klavierübung* in reference to the successful publication of Johann Kuhnau's partitas and sonatas. He also followed the example of his predecessor, cautiously exploring self-publishing, and recruiting colleagues from outside Leipzig to market the work further afield.[99]

By initially bringing the partitas out linked to trade fairs, and by giving the work a title that promised accessibility, he was aiming for a wide public. Simple keyboard pieces were always easiest to sell, and Bach wanted to capitalise on his reputation as a keyboard virtuoso. In this venture, with a sudden burst of bourgeois business acumen, the composer determined to leave nothing to chance. However, the music did not turn out to be simple: when all six partitas were published as a collection in 1731, Louise Adelgunde Victorie Kulmus gave her fiancé, the poet Gottsched, her first

Bach's first venture into publishing: the title page of partita BWV 825. Bach first published his music himself for the sake of caution.

impressions of Bach's 'Opus 1': 'The extremely ingenious keyboard pieces by Bach . . . are as difficult as they are beautiful. Though I may have played them ten times over, I still seem to myself a beginner in performing them.'[100]

When Bach published a second part of the *Klavierübung* in 1735, accessibility for amateur players was no longer his prime concern. Instead, he was anxious to introduce his public to all fields of keyboard music systematically. The partitas are followed in Bach's characteristic manner by an example of a concerto *to the Italian taste* (BWV 971) and an overture *in the French style* (BWV 831). In the third part of the *Klavierübung*, published in 1739 with a title page hardly concealing Bach's new status as court composer of Saxony, he turns to organists. The cycle is book-ended with a prelude and fugue (BWV 552), framing *on the Catechism hymns and other sacred songs* (BWV 669–689) and four duets (BWV 802–805). This publication imitates the *livres d'orgue* so popular in France.

The final part of the *Klavierübung*, published about 1742, is again dedicated to the keyboard and contains the *Goldberg Variations* (BWV 988). According to Johann Nicolaus Forkel, Bach's pupil Johann Gottlieb Goldberg was required to play these to the insomniac Count Hermann Carl von Keyserling during his sleepless nights. Perhaps the polonaise-like character of the aria, which begins and ends the variations, refers to the Royal Polish and Electoral Saxon court.

The *Goldberg Variations* are usually considered the final part of the *Piano Practice*. Perhaps Bach also wanted to include the second part of the *Well-tempered Clavier* and the *Art of the Fugue* in the collection, but he failed to deliver these pieces to the printer in time. In any case, Bach was eager, in later life, to integrate his piano and organ pieces into larger collections.

Bach was marketing not only his printed music, but keyboard works by Wilhelm Friedemann and the composer Conrad Friedrich Hurlebusch of Hamburg, his relation Johann Gottfried Walther's musical lexicon, and a *basso continuo* manual by Johann David Heinichen, Kapellmeister of Dresden. He also called on the aid of his

The aria *Bist du bei mir* BWV 508, from the *Klavierbüchlein* for Anna Magdalena Bach begun in 1725, in her own handwriting.

wife to make copies or transcriptions of his chamber music.[101] Finally, he also hired out musical instruments and provided technical information on the development of such new instruments as the viola pomposa and the fortepiano. A set of 14 canons on the first eight fundamental notes of the aria from the *Goldberg Variations* BWV 1087, was found only recently as an appendix to his own handwritten copy of that work.

Life must still have been very busy in the Bach household, even when the elder sons gradually left home to take up appointments elsewhere. Bach still had a large number of pupils, and many may not just have learnt from him but provided him with ideas in their turn. For instance, we find one Jakob von Stähelin, a member of the *Collegium Musicum* and a friend of the older Bach sons; this same Stähelin is known to history as the translator of *Saxe galante* by Carl Ludwig von Pollnitz,[102] published anonymously as 'a racy celebration of the heroic deeds of love performed by Augustus the Strong, with the obituary of the late Augustus' (he had died in 1733).[103] In 1735, this embroiled the translator into trouble with the Saxon censorship authorities. It is intriguing that Bach, who had just dedicated the *Kyrie* and *Gloria* of the *B-minor Mass* to Augustus the Strong's successor, was provided with racy gossip by his sons and the members of the *Collegium*.

We would not know much about Bach's everyday life in Leipzig, were it not for the composer's younger cousin Johann Elias Bach, who from 1737 to 1742 was living with the Bach family as tutor and secretary. His books of sketches and correspondence provide some touching and interesting details while hardly changing our image of Bach. Johann Sebastian, he writes, receives a present of game from Weissenfels; he likes wine and brandy. Anna Magdalena loves her husband, she likes yellow carnations, and wishes for a songbird, a linnet; in the summer of 1741, she falls seriously ill and can 'neither sit up nor lie down', so that her husband has to be summoned home urgently from his visit to Carl Philipp Emanuel, who was appointed chamber harpsichordist to Frederick the Great about this time.[104]

On 2 November 1748, Bach wrote to his cousin Johann Elias: *Most Noble and Most Esteemed Cousin, that you and also your dear wife are still well I am assured by the agreeable note I received from you yesterday accompanying the excellent little cask of wine you sent me, for which I send you herewith the thanks I owe you. It is, however, greatly to be regretted that the little cask was damaged, either by being shaken up in the wagon or in some other way, for when it was opened for the usual customs inspection here it was almost two-thirds empty, and according to the inspector's report contained no more than six quarts, and it is a pity that even the least drop of this noble gift of God should have been spilled . . .[105]*

Bach goes on to invite his cousin to the wedding of his *daughter Liesschen to the new organist in Naumburg, Mr Altnickol.* He closes: *Although my honoured Cousin kindly offers to oblige with more of the liquor, I must decline his offer on account of the excessive expenses here. For since the carriage charges cost 16 groschen for the carrier, the delivery man 2 groschen, the customs inspector 2 groschen, the inland duty 5 groschen 3 pfennig, and the general duty 3 groschen, my honoured Cousin can judge for himself that each quart cost me almost 5 groschen, which for a present is really too expensive.* Peter Schickele used this pedantic text as the basis for his irreverent *Bach: Portrait.*

Bach's middle Leipzig period receives less attention than any other part of his life, although it was at this time that he wrote such famous works as the *Kyrie* and *Gloria* of the *B-minor Mass*, the *Christmas Oratorio*, the *Peasant Cantata*, the *Italian Concerto* and the

Goldberg Variations. Yet in two respects it was a very productive time in which Bach clarified his aims. First, particularly in the four parts of the *Klavierübung*, he prepared the ground for his late work which, even if not esoteric or difficult, expresses the very essence of music. Second, Bach joined the debate over correct musical 'taste': his compositions of the time set new standards of sophistication and might well have been designed to give German music a voice in 'the European concert', a voice that laid down guidelines for the next generation of Haydn, Mozart and Beethoven.

The *Klavierübung* begins with a sequence of suites quizzically described by Bach as *Galanterien* (gallantries). Some of these works are strongly emotional, some are almost character pieces, but they are very strictly constructed. This is music which Schumann, the composer of the *Kreisleriana*, had he come upon it, might have liked even better than the much-admired *Well-Tempered Clavier.*

Bach makes it clear that he *could* write differently, but did not want to, in the second part of the *Klavierübung*. Here he compares his own ideas of form with a concerto *to the Italian taste* – a work that even his sternest critic, Johann Adolph Scheibe, described as 'a perfect model of a well-designed solo concerto'.[106]

Glenn Gould, the 20th-century Canadian pianist renowned for his interpretation of the *Goldberg Variations*, dismissed this as 'the sort of music Bach's sons wanted him to write'. Admittedly one may wonder whether Bach fully identified with this cheerful piece, or whether it was principally intended to serve as evidence of his musical skill. The style of the third part of the *Klavierübung* certainly gives such an impression. It begins in festive, even majestic tones, with a prelude in the rhythm of the French overture, but it is followed by chorale arrangements of incredible compositional difficulty. It is as if Bach wanted to continue along the lines of his *Orgelbüchlein*, whose style is retained here only in a few pieces which may be of earlier date. But the lyricism omnipresent in the earlier work, for all its contrapuntal severity, is now replaced by an uncompromising approach to musical organisation of a kind found only occasionally in the *Orgelbüchlein* – for instance in *Das alte Jahr vergangen ist (The old year now has passed away)*, BWV 614.

In this respect, the chorale *Vater unser im Himmelreich (Our Father which art in Heaven)*, BWV 682, headed *à 2 Clav. Et Pedal e Canto fermo in Canone*, is outstanding. Bach presents a setting with three obbligato parts that is already difficult and intriguing enough, with a complex mixture of rhythm and individual melodic developments and imposes a *cantus firmus* not in a single part but as a two-part canon. The astonishing result is a piece as bizarre as it is complex in structure; it cannot have been much to the taste of the majority of 'those gentlemen the organists' whom Johann Elias Bach addresses as its natural recipients in an advance announcement of this work.[107]

If Bach is establishing a link with the *Orgelbüchlein* in the chorale arrangements of the third part of the *Klavierübung*, then its duets may be seen, in much the same way, as a continuation of the earlier two-part *Inventions*.

Bach's musical rhetoric and symbolic forms of representation in these individual pieces and in the arrangement of an entire cycle are theologically intriguing. Was Bach linking the series of natural numbers with the Imitation of Christ (2), the Trinity (3), the points of the compass (4), the wounds of Christ (5), the petitions of the Lord's Prayer (7), the Mosaic commandments (10) and so on? Was he actually spelling out the name of the Saviour in-line with the numerical placing of letters in the German alphabet ($C + H + R + I + S + T + U + S = 3 + 8 + 17 + 9 + 18 + 19 + 20 + 18$), in an identifiable sequence of 112 notes or bars? Since Bach did occasionally resort to such ingenuity, there are some grounds for supposing that he indulged in calculations of this kind.

There has been considerable speculation on the basis of these ideas, which were first proposed by the theologian and Bach scholar Friedrich Smend.[108] Such notions gratify the author's[109] own search

CHORALE ARRANGEMENTS

for meaning rather than casting any light on Bach's manner of composition.[110] Constantly looking for B – A – C – H in the works of Bach is not very much more productive, since that chromatic sequence is practically unavoidable in certain keys, and is frequently also found in music written before Bach's time. To echo the words of his son Wilhelm Friedemann, Bach would have been 'a fool'[111] to keep scribbling his 'musical name' everywhere.

Finally, it must be asked whether works always gain in meaning if we take symbolic numbers into account, or whether they may not actually lose by it. Philipp Spitta has described it as an 'artistic whim' that in the opening chorus of the cantata *Du sollst Gott deinen Herren lieben (Thou shalt love the Lord thy God)* Bach did not arrange the chorale tune *Dies sind die heil'gen zehn Gebot (These are the sacred ten commandments)* to follow the normal run of the wording, but in what sounds like arbitrary order. 'Neither a poetic nor a musical reason for this procedure can be found!'[112] But we now know the reason: ten commandments, ten entrances of the trumpet.

The *Goldberg Variations*, which are matched historically only by Beethoven's *Diabelli Variations*, are no less intrically devised than the Catechism chorales: to mention only one factor in the order he followed, Bach composed variations 3, 6, 9, 12, 15, 18, 21, 24 and 27 as a canon at the unison, the second, the third, the fourth, the fifth, and so on. But this structure is softened by the songlike, dancing tone he imparts to the work. In the final variation he unites the tunes of two popular songs, *Ich bin so lang nicht bei dir g'west (It is so long since I saw you)* and *Kraut und Rüben haben mich vertrieben (Cabbage and turnips have driven me off)*, in a quodlibet.

Quodlibet is the playful combination of different songs as students played them already in the 14th century. The last movement of the *Goldberg Variations* is a rare example of a purely instrumental quodlibet, though a startling quodlibet appears in Biber's orchestra piece, *La Battaglio*.

While Bach was setting out along an increasingly steep path with the *Klavierübung*, he moved on more level ground in the secular cantatas of his middle Leipzig period. This was necessary to achieve the very public success he had enjoyed for years as director of the *Collegium Musicum*, particularly in the homage music written for the electoral house of Saxony. Refuting Johann Adolph Scheibe's polemic against Bach, Lorenz Mizler, one of Bach's pupils, wrote in 1739 of the cantata composed the previous year, *Willkommen, ihr herrschenden Götter der Erde* (*Welcome, ye ruling gods of earth*), BWV Anh 13, to a text by Gottsched and written for the wedding of Princess Maria Amalia of Dresden: 'But if Mr Bach at times writes the inner parts more fully than other composers, he has taken as his model the music of 20 or 25 years ago. He can write otherwise, however, when he wishes to. Anyone who heard the music that was performed by the students at the Easter Fair in Leipzig last year, in the Most High Presence of his Royal Majesty of Poland, which was composed by Kapellmeister Bach, must admit that it was written entirely in accordance with the latest taste, and was approved by everyone. So well does the Kapellmeister know how to suit himself to his listeners.'[113]

Unfortunately the music described in this passage has not survived. But the secular cantatas that have come down to us confirm Bach's ability to write in a generally lighter style, which can be described with some accuracy on the basis of contemporary notions. In his theory of poetry, Gottsched distinguishes between a 'high', a 'middle' and a 'low' style. Scheibe adopts these terms in the field of musical aesthetics, not exactly to do away with the old concepts of 'church', 'chamber' and 'theatrical' styles, but to relate their application to various genres. Viewed in parallel, these two systems of classification cast a helpful light on Bach's position in the aesthetic discussions of his time.

The 'high' style was distinguished by its elevated, pathetic or tragic manner; the poetics of the time link it particularly with themes from classical antiquity. In music, it was retained in essence for sacred compositions: in this sense, Bach's Leipzig cantatas and *Passions* follow both the 'church' style and the 'high' style.

According to contemporary literary theory, the 'middle' style was suitable for modern bourgeois tragedy, serious drama and comedies of feeling. There are strong parallels with Bach's secular cantatas, most of which he called *dramma per musica*, and the connection with the 'chamber' style is obvious, since the works concerned were almost all intended for the bourgeois *Collegium Musicum*. At this time, concepts such as 'beauty' or 'charm' were chosen to describe the 'middle' or 'chamber' style, and they could well be applied to Bach's secular cantatas that have come down to us.

In literary aesthetics, the 'low' style was suitable for comedy. In terms of musical aesthetics, it corresponds to the 'theatrical' style that Bach occasionally used in his secular cantatas. Before attending an opera in the capital, he is said to have asked his eldest son: *Friedemann, shall we not listen to those nice little Dresden songs again?*[114] It does not sound as if Bach identified with such a style. He is far more theatrical in his sacred dramas, those cantatas that evoke the terrors of the Last Judgement, such as *Wachet! Betet! Betet! Wachet!* (*Watch! Pray! Pray! Watch!*) BWV 70,[115] or the *Passions*. Such works have, at most, a very tenuous connection with this 'low' style.

It is easy to see what the 'middle' or 'chamber' style may have meant to Bach from the music of two congratulatory cantatas written in 1733: *Herkules auf dem Scheidewege* (*Hercules at the crossroads*) BWV 213, and *Tönet, ihr Pauken! Erschallet, Trompeten!* (*Sound, drums! Ring out, trumpets!*) BWV 214. This music is also known to us from the *Christmas Oratorio*, for which he 'parodied' it, using it as the setting for different words: *Tönet, ihr Pauken! Erschallet, Trompeten! Klingende Saiten, erfüllen die Luft* (*Sound, drums! Ring out, trumpets! Sounding strings, fill the air*), becomes *Jauchzet, frohlocket, auf, preiset die Tage, rühmet was heute der Höchste getan!* (*Rejoice and be glad, praise the day, praise what the Highest has done on this day!*). Hercules's aria *Ich will dich nicht hören, ich will dich nicht wissen, verworfene Wollust, ich kenne dich nicht!* (*I will not hear you, I will not know you, depraved lust, I know you not!*) becomes, in the new text: *Bereite dich Zion mit zärtlichen Trieben, den Schönsten, den Liebsten bald bei dir zu seh'n!* (Prepare ye, O Zion, with loving affection, the fairest, the dearest, to see with you soon!).

The opening chorus is 'revised'. Bach takes the command 'Sound, drums!' literally in musical terms. The kettledrums, which can produce only a single interval of a fourth, are incorporated to provide thematic material; 'their' interval becomes the basis of the entire movement. The choral part also contains less striking imitations in the words *Singet itzt Lieder / Lasset das Zagen* (Now sing songs / Hesitate no longer), and *Königin lebe / Dienet dem Höchsten!* (Long live the Queen! / Serve ye the Highest). But this is hardly comparable with the great chorale fugues and elaborate *cantus firmus* arrangements which make many of the church cantatas tend towards the high and elevated style. Instead, the writing is homophonic for long passages, so that the main part can always be easily heard; the articulation of the singing voices is naturalistic; the various rhythmic and metric phrases are constructed and organised so that the whole form can be followed easily; its general tendency is comparable to the structure of a dance or song. The criterion for such simplicity is not the use of concertante form in itself but an ability to manage that form easily.

The aria *Ich will dich nicht hören / Bereite dich Zion* (I will not hear you / Prepare, O Zion) confirms this impression. Bach is almost more careful in the 'parody' than in the original version to bring out the meaning of the text, stressing key statements such as the words *The fairest, the dearest*, a tuneful 16-bar ritornello that he constructs is a model of symmetry. The cradle song which begins identically in both versions, *Schlafe mein Liebster* (Sleep now, my dearest), stands, *pars pro toto*, for an elaborate but at the same time evocative and immediately catchy treatment of melody. Works and parts of works like those described are useful in helping to assess the music of Bach as court composer, and show that the music belongs to a 'middle' style, transcending the then popular polarities of 'learned' or '*galant*'.

This tendency to a 'middle' style is also evident in the great sacred work based on the two works of homage music mentioned above, with sections taken from other secular and sacred cantatas: the six-part *Christmas Oratorio* performed over Christmas and New Year 1734–5. In compiling such a work, Bach had plenty of suitable choruses and arias for 'parody' ready to hand. However, he needed to compose new music for the main liturgical pillars of the oratorio: the Biblical Christmas story and the chorales relating to it. Traditional Christmas music may have been involved, too; in new sections like the *Sinfonia*, Bach shows a liking for gentle, traditional 'pastorale' style, creating a counterbalance to the confessional music of his two *Passions*. As Lorenz Mizler said, Bach could fit his music to his listeners.

Three particular factors may have induced him to lean so heavily on 'parody' in composing the *Christmas Oratorio*. First, 'parody' enabled him to offer the people of Leipzig a great sacred work without having to compose it entirely from scratch. Second, and perhaps even during the actual composition of the originals, he may have seen it as a way to preserve his music from oblivion by placing it in a durable, relevant context, something that the *occasional* nature of the secular versions could not provide.[116] Third, the works parodied in this creative phase of Bach's career have a lightness of touch that lets their revision appear relatively easy. However, Bach steers clear of anything *too* light: at the last minute he rejected the closing gavotte-like chorus of the Hercules cantata as a model for the opening chorus of the fifth part of the *Christmas Oratorio*, even though he already had the new text for the movement in front of him.

Bach even has some examples of the *galant* style in its narrower sense. In the aria *Fromme Musen, meine Glieder, singt nicht längst bekannte Lieder!* (*Pious Muses, ah, my members, sing no songs long known of old!*) from the homage cantata BWV 214, he was forced, not least by the text, into using a style that matched it, although it was not so suitable to accompany the 'happy shepherds' to the crib in its 'parody' in the *Christmas Oratorio*.

Other examples occur in the two cantatas written on knightly estates, *Angenehmes Wiederau (Pleasant Wiederau)* BWV 30a, and *Mer Hahn en neue Oberkeet (The new lord of the manor)*, humorously interrupted in the *Peasant Cantata*. About 1742, Bach performed what, to the ears of the time, was a very modern church work, Giovanni Battista Pergolesi's *Stabat Mater*, although with a German text and the addition of a viola part.

In Bach's instrumental music examples of *galant* style appear in

Giovanni Battista Pergolesi (1710–36) became famous for his 1733 intermezzo, *La serva padrona*, and later throughout all Europe for his *Stabat Mater*. The fact that Bach reworked the latter piece around 1746–7 for a church performance proves that he was interested in both the *stilo antico* and in contemporary music.

the slow movements of the flute sonata of 1747, dedicated to Frederick the Great against the background of the *Musical Offering*. He did not adopt the style merely on this occasion, as we can see from the B minor BWV 1030 flute sonata, written some time earlier, and the Prelude in D major BWV 874 from the second part of the *Well-Tempered Clavier*, written in 1742. This part includes many older pieces; Bach did not plan it as the first part. Even his more severe keyboard works show features reminiscent of the *galant* style, although with a melancholy turn, for instance in the 25th of the *Goldberg Variations* or the *Canon Per Augmentationem in contrario Motu* from the *Art of Fugue*.

How did the 'court composer' present himself in his dedicatory work, the *Kyrie* and *Gloria* of the *B-minor Mass*? The initial style of *Kyrie* is not entirely original, but typical of the genre, very similar, for instance, to a Mass by Bach's contemporary Johann Hugo von Wilderer. Bach had copied it at Dresden and may have used it as a background model for the whole of the first *Kyrie*.[117] In the second *Kyrie*, however, he went his own way, composing one of his rare vocal movements in the manner of the *stile antico*, almost like

A view, looking straight from Bach's lodgings, of the *galant* society of Leipzig: the promenade. Coloured engraving by Bergmüller from a drawing by Johann August Rosmäsler, 1777

Palestrina, although utilising the harmonic and chromatic possibilities of his own time. Perhaps this was by way of telling the court of Saxony: 'I can master your modern style very well, but when it comes to setting the Catholic Mass the old style must be preserved too.'

The more Bach's works achieved public acclaim, the more criticism they attracted as well. From 1737 to 1739, this opprobrium was expressed, above all, by Johann Adolph Scheibe. Scheibe, a native of Leipzig, moved to Hamburg in 1736, in order to publish a weekly journal, the *Critischer Musicus*, under Telemann's supervision. His great admiration for Bach did not prevent him using his journal for the new taste, based on the aesthetic of natural imitation, in the spirit of the French Enlightenment. He wanted music to imitate nature, and thus he saw song as predominant. On 14 May 1737, he wrote of Bach: 'This great man would be the admiration of whole nations if he had more amenity, if he did not take away the natural element in his pieces by giving them a turgid and confused style, and if he did not darken their beauty by an excess of art. [. . .] All the voices must work with each other and be of equal difficulty, and none of them can be recognised as the principal voice. In short, he is in music what Mr von Lohenstein was in poetry. Turgidity has led them both from the natural to the artificial, and from the lofty to the sombre; and in both, one admires the onerous labour and uncommon effort – which, however, are vainly employed, since they conflict with Nature' (in the second edition Scheibe says: 'against reason').[118]

Scheibe repeated these criticisms several times, and Bach seems to have taken them very seriously. He found a supporter in Magister Johann Abraham Birnbaum, lecturer on law, philosophy and rhetoric at Leipzig University. However, the two valiant little treatises that Birnbaum immediately produced in defence hardly presented an effective aesthetic counter-attack. If a draft letter from Johann Elias Bach has been correctly interpreted, Johann Sebastian had at least one of these treatises printed. Sometimes it seems that the composer himself is speaking, although in general he naturally did not or could not direct the author's pen. One can hardly reproach Birnbaum for being unable to press Scheibe hard in argument – the trend of the times was too obviously going Scheibe's way. How would Carl Philipp Emanuel have felt had he been obliged to defend his father in this situation? At the time, as a precursor of the new taste, he was writing his first *galant* flute sonatas, and a little later he published keyboard sonatas in the modern style, dedicating them pointedly to Frederick the Great. While Carl Philipp Emanuel's father was not a *galant* composer, he was *the* master of the *galant* style.

The universalist: the late Leipzig period

TO 1750

In October 1739, the Leipzig newspapers announced that 'the Royal
Polish and Electoral Saxon Court Composer Bach has resumed the
direction of the *Collegium Musicum* in Zimmermann's coffee house.'[119]
For two years, he had left it in the hands of Carl Gotthelf Gerlach,
who acted as a 'deputy'. Bach's 'resignation' may have been as a
result of the dispute of the prefects but now he took office again for
a further two to five years, and immediately had a 'solemn serenade'
performed for the birthday celebrations of the king and elector.
Familiar as these activities were to him, a new, final creative phase
was already taking shape: almost on the same day and at the same
time, Bach announced the third part of the *Klavierübung*, including
the Catechism chorales.

In 1739 also, Johann Mattheson (1684–1761) published his definitive work on music theory, the *Vollkommenen Capellmeister*. This
great Hamburg authority mentioned and quoted Bach in connection
with all species of counterpoint: fugue, double fugue, circular fugue
and so on. Admittedly, Mattheson's observations are lengthy and
admiring, but they are also mocking of Magister Birnbaum's efforts
to present Bach a master of melody too, as a 'master in all things'.
He writes explicitly: 'Of double fugues with three subjects, nothing
has come out in engraving as far as I know except my own work,
under the name *of Der Wohlklingende Fingersprache*, parts one and
two in 1735 and 1737, which out of modesty I will refrain from
recommending to anyone, but I could perhaps wish to see something
of the kind see the light of day by the famous Herr Bach in Leipzig,

a great master of the fugue. This deficiency is sufficient evidence on the one hand of the negligence and decline of strict contrapuntalists, and on the other of the small demand for such instructive material by ignorant organists and composers of the present day.'[120]

Bach would hardly have been flattered by Mattheson's remarks, and probably noticed the sting in the tail. He certainly did not see himself as merely the provider of 'instructive material' which failed to achieve wide distribution. Far from being in decline, he was busy with the work designed to highlight once more his skill in the art of counterpoint in, effectively, a kind of fifth part of the *Klavierübung*. His heirs later published what he completed as the *Art of Fugue*. More appropriately, it might have been called the 'Art of Counterpoint' or 'Ars Canonica',[121] as it is less concerned with the fugue itself than with the problem of how to deal with a subject in a richness of treatments. In the third part of the *Klavierübung*, the tune of whatever chorale was being set had served as the *soggetto* or subject; in the fourth part, the *Goldberg Variations* served as the bass foundation of a single aria on which all the 30 variations were based. Now, Bach went a step further in the concentration of his musical material. His point of departure was no longer identifiable melody, but a sequence of notes constructed solely for the purpose of development, a sequence that cannot be described as abstract but was carefully 'constructed' in every other particular.

The *Art of Fugue* was neither Bach's last work nor, in any real sense, a musical will and testament. Death did not take the pen from his hand as he wrote the last fugue; there is good reason to suppose that it was already in existence, however incomplete, in 1748–9. Once completed, the body of it was intended to be part of the entire *Art of Fugue* project: the *soggetto* of the *Art of Fugue* does not appear at the stage of its composition in which it has come down to us, and it is mere supposition that the subject was intended to be the fourth theme of a quadruple fugue at some further point in the course of the piece. Instead, a theme developed from the notes B – A – C – H is strikingly prominent. It seems possible, though not inevitable, that it was to be part of the sequence later called the *Art of Fugue*: for Bach to refer to himself directly by using the B – A – C – H sequence indicated a subjectivity in blatant contrast to the pure structured hopes of the *Art of Fugue*.

Of course, Carl Philipp Emanuel lent his express authority to the story in the *Obituary*, and Wilhelm Friedemann confirmed it. But C P E Bach had been responsible for the lacunae in his edition of the work, such as the printing of one of the counterpoints twice. The posthumous printing of the *Art of Fugue* suggests that the bereaved family wanted to show the greatest respect for what there was of the work, passing it on to posterity as something unique, but perhaps lacked an understanding of the actual state of the composition. This is not surprising, for Bach himself altered his plans over time, and may not have ever come to any definitive conclusion. After all, in the last decade of his life, so many aspects of counterpoint fascinated him that individual projects must all be regarded as 'works in progress'.

Today, most experts believe that Bach composed the *Art of the Fugue* for keyboard, though over the course of music history the piece has been arranged for many other instruments as well, the most extreme example being Wolgang Gräser's 1927 version for a large orchestra with trumpets and trombones.

About 1742, closely connected with the Catechism chorales and the *Goldberg Variations*, Bach wrote down 12 movements of what would later become the *Art of Fugue* in fair copy. This shows that he had been concerned with the project for some time, and perhaps wanted to 'set' some of it. Not long afterwards, about 1746–7, he returned to the work, adding two more movements to the growing corpus.

Roughly contemporaneous manuscript collections containing the organ chorales BWV 651–668 (most of them composed considerably earlier) and their often much older models also included preludes and fugues from the second part of the *Well-Tempered Clavier* BWV 870–893, some of them transposed *ad hoc* into suitable keys. In the field of vocal music, Bach was deliberately turning his mind to the *stile antico*, making a copy of Palestrina's famous *Missa sine nomine* as an example. What may sound like a dry technical exercise found expression a few years later in a way that attracted public attention. On 11 May 1747, a report in the *Berlinische Nachrichten* read:

'We hear from Potsdam that last Sunday the famous Kapellmeister from Leipzig, Mr Bach, arrived with the intention of hearing the excellent Royal music at that place. In the evening, at about the time when the regular chamber music in the Royal apartments usually begins, His Majesty was informed that Kapellmeister Bach had arrived at Potsdam and was waiting in His Majesty's antechamber for His Majesty's most gracious permission to listen to the music. His August Self immediately gave orders that Bach be admitted, and went, at his entrance, to the so-called "forte and piano", condescending also to play, in person and without any preparation, a theme to be executed by Kapellmeister Bach in a fugue. This was done so happily by the aforementioned Kapellmeister that not only His Majesty was pleased to show his satisfaction thereat, but also all present were seized with astonishment. Mr Bach found the subject propounded to him so exceedingly beautiful that he intends to set it down on paper in a regular fugue and have it engraved on copper.

'On Monday, the famous man was heard on the organ in the church of the Holy Ghost at Potsdam, and earned general acclaim from the auditors attending in great number. In the evening, His Majesty charged him again with the execution of a fugue, in six parts, which he accomplished just as skilfully as on the previous occasion, to the pleasure of His Majesty and to general admiration.'[122]

This article, reprinted in the presses of Hamburg, Magdeburg and other cities, is an instance of a public relations strategy which even Mattheson could not have bettered. Bach arrived quietly, a potential admirer of the modern taste which the King of Prussia, then aged 35, wished his Kapelle to adopt. He goes home, his head held high, brilliantly successful as a representative of the older style.

According to an account by Forkel deriving from Wilhelm Friedemann, Bach first improvised on the new fortepiano built by Gottfried Silbermann before asking the monarch to give him a theme. Frederick would hardly have given 'his' theme in the highly polished form that Bach later set down on paper. It is impossible to ascertain whether it was all his own in the first place, or whether his court musicians had a hand in it, or indeed whether it originated with Bach himself by way of Carl Philipp Emanuel as court harpsichordist. But Bach certainly did not set out for Potsdam unprepared: in view of his determined efforts to obtain a Saxon title it would not be surprising if he wanted to be well regarded by the rising star of Europe. His own elector, fighting in alliance with Austria, had just lost the Second Silesian War, and all eyes were turned to Prussia.

Gottfried Silbermann (1683–1753) worked primarily on the development of the pianoforte. According to Bach's pupil Johann Friedrich Agricola, after playing on one of Silbermann's pianos, the master complained that the high pitches were too weak and the mechanics not easy enough. Silbermann subsequently spent years trying to improve the instrument, and during his visit in Potsdam, Bach found that the updated instrument suited his taste entirely. Bach performed at least three times on organs from Silbermann's workshop: in 1725 and 1731 in Dresden at the *Sophienkirche*, and in 1736 at the *Frauenkirche*.

With Potsdam in mind, as soon as he returned from Berlin, Bach immediately set to work on an opus in several parts based on the *Thema regium*. Calling it the *Musical Offering*, he had it engraved and presented it to the king. He wrote down a three-part ricercar based on his improvisation, composed a new six-part one, and in addition ten skilful canons on the royal theme. He also composed a four-movement trio sonata on the 'Prussian' theme for flute, violin and *basso continuo* paying tribute to Frederick the Great's flute-playing and his musical tastes.

Before the first edition of a hundred copies was sold out, Bach had already finished two comparable works: the six organ trios worked up from older originals for the publisher Johann Georg Schübler, BWV 645–650, and the *Canonical Variations on the Christmas Hymn: Vom Himmel hoch da komm ich her (I come to you from heaven on high)*, BWV 769. The latter, together with the somewhat enigmatic canon BWV 1076, was Bach's presentation on joining the 'Corresponding Society of the Musical Sciences', the society founded by Lorenz Christoph Mizler in 1738. The members were also interested in 'philosophy, mathematics, oratory and poetry', and were expected to produce a learned but not dry-as-dust work every year. Bach did not actually become a member of the society until 1747, and was the 14th to join, adding his name to, amongst others, Georg Philipp Telemann, Gottfried Heinrich Stölzel, George Frideric Handel and Karl Heinrich Graun. Interestingly, 14 is also 'his' number if the name B – A – C – H is calculated in terms of the numerical alphabet.

In 1734, Mizler had dedicated his thesis to both Mattheson and Bach. Having read mathematics, music and philosophy at Leipzig University, and translated into German the most famous manual of counterpoint, Johann Joseph Fux's *Gradus ad Parnassum*, he regarded the study of music as a philosophical exercise. By the time he had recruited Bach to his society he had long since moved from Leipzig. By this time it is not clear how much public interest the society still aroused.

Bach turned back to the *Art of Fugue*, presumably in the first half of 1748. Apparently, he intended to have the piece published but, just as he was sending revised versions of the first movements to the engraver, he was overcome by a wish to construct another, even more comprehensive 'masterplan'. This included simple fugues on the theme and its inversion, counter-fugues on the theme and its inversion, double, triple and quadruple fugues on the theme and on one to three further themes, mirror fugues (where the second part is a 'mirror image' of the first on the horizontal axis) and canons. All this demanded adjustments and new compositions.

Indeed, there were so many complications that he let the project fall fallow once more, never guessing that death would prevent its completion, confronting his sons with the task of making a work fit to print out of what was left. Bach's last great work was not the *Art of Fugue* but the *B-minor Mass*.[123]

There may have been external reasons for the intensive work that Bach did on the Mass between the summer of 1748 and the autumn of 1749, making the incomplete piece dedicated to Elector Friedrich August of Saxony in 1733, consisting only of the *Kyrie* and *Gloria*, into a complete work by adding a *Credo*, *Sanctus*, *Osanna* with *Benedictus*, and *Agnus Dei*. The court church in Dresden was about to be consecrated, and this was an important occasion for Bach to provide music as court composer. Bach composed additional sections for the *Credo* in *stile antico*. All the other remaining new material was probably adapted from earlier works. For the *Sanctus*, Bach resorted to a separate piece dating from 1724, while borrowing other numbers from material such as the secular homage cantatas of the 1730s. The *Osanna*, for instance, was originally in the chorus *Es lebe der König, der Vater im Lande (Long live the King, father of the land)* BWV Anh 11, which had already served as the model for a musical 'parody', *Preise dein Glücke, gesegnetes Sachsen (Praise thy good fortune, blessed Saxony)* BWV 215.

While working on the *B-minor Mass* and the *Art of Fugue*, Bach was also participating as a non-speaking actor in a public drama: the choice of his successor. On 8 June 1749, Gottlob Harrer, Kapellmeister to Count Heinrich von Brühl, the Prime Minister of Saxony, auditioned at the Three Swans Inn for the post of Kantor. The Leipzig council was acceding to a request from the all-powerful minister; it could hardly do otherwise, since the city owed the elector enormous sums, which he owed to the King of Prussia as war reparations. The audition did not take place on Bach's own territory, in one of the main city churches, but in a concert hall. Perhaps Bach was regarded at this time as ailing, but he was hardly seriously ill and certainly not enfeebled by old age. It is not known whether he was offended, for it was by no means uncommon for the holder of a position to look for his successor during his own lifetime. If Bach did feel injured, he may have given vent to his feelings rather subtly. In the cantata *Geschwinde, ihr wirbelnden Winde* (*Fast, fast, ye whirling winds*) BWV 201, revived in 1749, he changed the name of the classically derived 'raging Orbilius' to *Birolius*. This invented name was probably a dig at Count Brühl.[124]

We can only speculate on the reasons behind this seemingly premature audition for the post of Kantor. Perhaps the minister wanted to rid himself of an unpopular music director. Perhaps he wanted to show the people of Leipzig what modern church music could be like. In any case, a few months later Mayor Horn complained in person that only too often 'miserable singers'[125] were sent to the church of St Nikolai as a result of administrative errors.

However, while Bach may not have appeared to perform his duties in the last decade of his life less diligently than before, there is much to suggest that he increasingly saw himself as a private person, endeavouring to complete his official duties as quickly as possible in order to have time to compose for himself, to complete his life's work, indeed to complete his own musical memorial.[126] By joining Mizler's society, Bach may finally have made it clear that he no longer regarded himself as a church official, or even as court composer, but as a musician whose only allegiance was to the art of music and to himself.

Bach was ready to defend the value of teaching music in schools, as is evident from his firm reaction to an anti-musical educational programme proposed in 1749 by the Rektor in Freiberg, Johann Gottlieb Biedermann. Biedermann, writing in learned Latin, propounded his theory that too much music-making debilitated the young and led them astray. Bach asked a fellow member of Mizler's society, Christoph Gottlieb Schröter, to write a rebuttal, in order to cleanse the Rektor's *Dreckohr* ('dirty ear', reversing the sound effect of *Rektor*). Bach, like Mozart after him, loved such wordplay. He himself had this response printed, although not entirely to the author's satisfaction, since Bach added some sharper remarks of his own.[127]

Bach could not participate personally in the ensuing discussion. After two eye operations – performed in late March and early April 1750 by the eye surgeon or 'oculist' John Taylor – he fell ill. Although the Berlin and Leipzig newspapers reported that Taylor's treatment of Bach had been successful, advanced cataracts were irreversible.

'Not only could he no longer use his eyes, but his whole system, which was otherwise thoroughly healthy, was completely overwhelmed by the operation and by the addition of harmful medicaments and other things, so that, thereafter, he was almost continuously ill for half a year. Ten days before his death his eyes suddenly seemed better, so that one morning he could see quite well again and could also again endure the light. But a few hours later he suffered a stroke; and this was followed by a raging fever, as a victim of which, despite every possible care given him by two of the most skilful physicians of Leipzig, on 28 July 1750, a little after a quarter to nine in the evening, in the 66th year of his life, he quietly and peacefully, by the merit of his Redeemer, departed this life.'[128]

The skill of Taylor, a highly regarded surgeon, has never really been in doubt. Bach's death was historically attributed to an infection of the wound that led to the stroke and fatal pneumonia as the direct cause of death. However, now it seems that Bach died not of the consequences of his cataract operation, but of diabetes.[129]

According to the preface to the *Art of Fugue*, Bach, who can hardly have regarded himself as mortally ill before his eye operation, is said to have dictated the chorale *Wenn wir im höchsten Nöten sind / Vor deinen Thron tret ich hiermit* (When we are in greatest need / With this before thy throne I come) BWV 668a on his deathbed. Even though this tale is thought to be a legend,[130] it is not mere obscurantism. Bach not only set the principles of the Christian faith to music but lived by them himself, as witnessed by such evidence as the entries in his three-volume Bible. Among them is a comment on Chronicles 5: 13, showing Bach making a close connection with his own life's work: *N.B. When devout music is performed, God and his grace are always present.*[131]

'A man, 67 years, Mr Johann Sebastian Bach, Kapellmeister and Kantor of the Thomas-Schule, died Tuesday. Four children. Hearse gratis,' runs the entry in the gravedigger's book for 30 July 1750.[132] The funeral took place at St John's cemetery, a ceremony appropriate to Bach's social standing. Anna Magdalena, pledging not to marry again, applied for the guardianship of her underage children Johann Christoph Friedrich, Johann Christian, Johanna Carolina and Regina Susanna, and received the usual half-year's grace. While she received only the smaller part of her husband's estate, which was estimated at less than 1,000 reichstalers, she suffered no direct want. She was described as an 'almswoman', making her not a beggar, but the widow of a city servant living on a small pension.

Few traces remain of Bach's civic or private life; just a few official documents, and a handful of personal letters. It is not known whether he ever reconciled himself to his situation in Leipzig, having

After Bach's death, his three youngest children with Anna Magdalena had very different lives. As a successful composer in London, Johann Christian (1735–82) made a great impression on the young Mozart, but after a full and active life died earlier than his three older and also successful brothers. The two youngest sisters faced an unhappy future: after their mother's death in 1760, they suffered material need. In 1800 the *Allgemeine Musikalische Zeitung* published an appeal on behalf of the only living survivor among Bach's children, Regina Susanna, then nearly 60 years old. Beethoven expressed his willingness to support the appeal 'before this Bach dies, before that Bach dries up' [literally, Bach = brook, stream].[133]

DEATH

The problem of the authentic likeness of Bach: this picture (now in private possession in the US), dating from 1748 and by Elias Gottlob Haussmann, who portrayed the notable personalities of Leipzig, shows signs of over-painting but is clearly better preserved than Haussmann's earlier version of 1746, now in the Leipzig Museum für Geschichte.

Four Bach portraits of doubtful authenticity. Clockwise from top left: an oil painting from the Städtisches Museum of Erfurt, ascribed to Joachim Ernst Rentsch; an oil painting by Johann Jakob Ihle assumed to be of Bach and painted c.1720, from the Bach House in Eisenach; a pastel in private possession in Eisenach, said on the grounds of oral tradition to have been painted by one of the Meiningen Bachs and to show J S Bach; an oil painting done as a free variation on the Haussmann picture, and making use of a portrait engraving by Samuel Gottlob Kütner.

complained so vehemently of it in his letter to Erdmann in 1730, or whether his constant disputes with the authorities stirred stronger feelings in him as the years went by or left him increasingly indifferent. In any case, little can be said about his 'nature'. He may well have been self-assured, ambitious, opinionated, quick-tempered; not necessarily a kindly man, but sociable and humorous. It would not be surprising if he had fits of melancholy – supposing he had time for them – given the many claims on him as a family man: the husband of two wives and father of 20 children, some of whom died in infancy while others grew up to be extremely musical, and he was also a host who entertained many musicians, including the very famous. He promoted the interests of his sons even if he may have been an impatient teacher to them and his other pupils. He was devout, but not only interested in theology, for he seems to have been an attentive observer of the religious events of his time. He was certainly aware of his own genius, and did not want to be misunderstood: his attempts to achieve social recognition are a thread running all through his life. His working stamina was extraordinary, and we owe many sublime musical experiences to it.

The mention of 'late work' is not particularly helpful: Bach's compositions after the end of the 1730s are not the quintessence or conclusion of his life's work but rather extend a single if important aspect of that work, making others not exactly disappear but retreat into the overall picture.

In his own creative music, he continued to be very much the Kantor and court composer, just as he was in his professional life. And the organist of the early years is still present. The ageing Bach did not close his mind to contemporary musical tastes, as evidenced by his readiness to adopt features of the *galant* style. It is abundantly obvious that Bach wanted to bring out the essence of music mainly through contrapuntal work.

The ideal goes back to the old composers of the Netherlands and the 'classic' vocal polyphony of Palestrina, by now considered to be the *stile antico*. The older Bach grew, the more he valued that art and paid tribute to it, especially in the *B-minor Mass*. He could draw on sources which had not yet dried up in the conservative church music of his time; his colleague as court composer in Dresden, Jan Dismas Zelenka, for instance, showed a predilection for traditional church music. Bach certainly committed himself more than his contemporaries did to transferring the *stile antico* to instrumental music, although here too he found a fellow enthusiast in Heinrich Bokemeyer, like him a member of Mizler's society.

According to Johann Gottfried Walther's musical lexicon, counterpoint in the widest sense is 'any harmonic combination' of several parts. The fact that this combination must be achieved in polyphonic obbligato writing marks Bach's style at every phase of his life. We come closer to the Bach of the late Leipzig period in a concept that his pupil Johann Philipp Kirnberger puts forward in his treatise *Die Kunst des reinen Satzes* (*The Art of Pure Writing*): 'There is perhaps in the whole science of writing nothing more difficult than this: not only to give each of the four voices its own flowing melody, but also to keep a uniform character in all, so that out of their union a single and perfect whole may arise. In this, the late Kapellmeister Bach in Leipzig perhaps excelled all the composers in the world.'[134]

Instrumental works that can be included in this context are several fugues from the *Well-Tempered Clavier*, such as the C-sharp minor and B-flat minor in Book I, and the E major and B major in Book II. The moniker ricercar for the three-part and six-part counterpoint of the *Musical Offering* is indicative: Bach is pointedly recalling older music. The same can be said of large parts of the *Art of Fugue*, beginning with *Contrapunctus 1*, which lends its character to the entire work. This is modelled on the instrumental ricercars by such 16th- and 17th-century composers as Adriaan Willaert and Girolamo Frescobaldi.[135]

In his later Leipzig period, Bach extended the ideal of pure polyphonic writing. The apogee of this is the canon, in which polyphony flowers from a single voice. In the Middle Ages, the

The 'royal theme' artistically developed: the canones diversi from the *Musical Offering*, engraved as a tribute to Frederick the Great.

three-part canon was regarded as the symbol of the Trinity; in the theological interpretation of music it also expressed perfection of musical form. For the connoisseur, a canon is especially fascinating if it is presented as a riddle or enigma: the composer presents but *one* voice, allowing the hearer to work out when and at what pitch the other voices will come in, whether they will follow the course of the first voice in augmented or diminished note values, in inversion or retrograde motion (the 'crab' canon or *cancrizans*).

The canons of the *Musical Offering* show their idiosyncrasies in their rubrics: the *Canon cancrizans* must be read both forwards and backwards; the *Canon per Augmentationem in contrario Motu*, with the second part running in inversion with doubled-note values; the *Canon per Tonos* rises a whole tone higher with each statement of the theme, only returning to the home key after the sixth rotation. *Ascendente Modulatione ascendat Gloria Regis* was a comment entered by Bach in the dedication copy: *May the King's fame ascend with the rising modulation*. Above the two last canons are the significant words: *Quaerendo invenietis* (*In searching lies discovery*).

The *Goldberg Variations* and canons used in the arrangements of the hymn *Vom Himmel hoch* and the *Art of Fugue* are less strikingly announced but are just as sophisticated. Although Bach spent many decades working on this material, special effects did not come of themselves. For instance, this is illustrated in the changes undergone by the canon in retrograde motion and augmentation from the *Art of Fugue*, from its first occurrence in writing to the time when it appeared in print. Of course, the same may be said of the fugues, which are full of all kinds of difficulties.

The 14 canons that Bach entered later in his manuscript copy of the *Goldberg Variations* give a glimpse of his compositional process. On the one hand, he tries to find out systematically, almost arithmetically, what can be done with a *soggetto*. On the other, he wants to make his results as cryptic and difficult to solve as possible.[136] Such ideas can come to obsess a musician: not only must *all come from one*, the *one* must also be found. A composer must find his 'philosopher's stone' before hiding it so effectively that only an expert can unearth it.

In their contrapuntal skill, the *Canonical Variations*, the *Musical Offering* and the *Art of Fugue* are of equal quality. However, if it is to be supposed that Bach was trying to capture the essence of music as expression as well as order, these three works, although characteristic of his last Leipzig period, are very different. The *Canonic*

Variations are somewhat brittle, and the *Kinderlied auf die Weihnacht Christi* (*Children's Hymn on the Birth of Christ*) by no means suits its title. The *Musical Offering* is a collection of traditional 'cabinet pieces'. Bach's problem here was how to create a musical universe from a strict canon to *galant* trio sonata, using a 'royal' theme that, by its nature, would dominate the writing.

By contrast, *Art of Fugue* was not a commissioned or occasional work; it is Bach's very philosophy of music. As such, its point of departure is not a theme, although it makes use of one, but the intention of making a statement of general relevance through music. Its modest theme only provides the material for building Bach's universal statement. The composer was not concerned to develop this theme through it, but to embody the very nature of it.

Bach's deliberate use of *Contrapunctus* and not 'fugue' in the *Art of Fugue* was with a view to the many kinds of counterpoint outlined by Walther in his lexicon, but also in the sense of 'harmonious writing', quite independent of the particular nature of the writing. If that writing was to be 'perfect',[137] as Magister Birnbaum claimed in principle for Bach's style, it meant not just in technique but equally in its very meaning. Only recently has the *Art of Fugue* been seen from this angle.

It is also concerned to a considerable extent with representing emotions and expressive characteristics, and with confronting features such as the French overture, the concerto, the use of cantus firmus, the invention, and so on, and there is no lack of stylistic and figurative factors in line with the ideas of musical rhetoric.[138]

A very progressive, dynamic understanding of form is evident in *Contrapunctus IV*, which was composed somewhat late. This looks to fugue or the sonata genre, even to modern ideas of composition, in which each piece embodies its own order, an order brought to life only in its subjective, expressive 'use' by both composer and audience.[139] In principle, this could also be applied to corresponding studies of the *Art of Fugue*. The 'prestabilised

The Enlightenment witnessed the coming of age of surgery in Europe; previously, it was perceived as little more than butchery. Ocular surgery was pioneered by the Frenchman Jacques Daviel (1696–1762), who performed the first successful cataract operations. His was success was emulated by the mountebank 'Chevalier' John Taylor (1703–72), who, whilst skilled in the operation to remove a hardened lens, was a shameless publicist and a showman, later alleged not only to have hastened Bach's blindness, but Handel's as well.

harmony' of which Gottfried Wilhelm Leibniz spoke is not only overthrown but put into a state of powerful flux.

It is not Bach's readiness to accept the *galant* style or the *Sturm und Drang* of his sons' generation that made him universal, but the perspectives that he opened up, looking far beyond that generation, even beyond Beethoven, Brahms, even to Arnold Schoenberg and Anton Webern, and into the future.

This art of 'pure' counterpoint engendered that of 'pure composition': not just purity of style but the wish to attain perfection itself, the quintessential lying beyond any particular forms and genres. Today, composers are still exploring the musical regions, world and empyreans that Bach mapped out.

Such a search for perfection must end in 'polystylistism', even disunity. In the *Art of Fugue*, Bach not only presented various possibilities of musical writing but conducted an open-ended dialectic with music. While Bach stands undisputedly at the top of the contrapuntalist tree, he is only a signpost on the way to goals that would be rediscovered by Mozart and Haydn in their chamber music. That is, a method of counterpoint that is no less syntactically logical than a purely contrapuntal one, but at the same time offers the composer the opportunity to steer the thematic process towards individual freedom.

It is easy to see why Bach not only composed some additional pieces before printing the *Art of Fugue* but also revised the endings of the three first *Contrapuncti* and extended them. The individual pieces could not end just because the rules of *counterpoint* dictate that they should, but because they are making for perorations determined by the *composer* independently of the rules. He needed to formulate these conclusions so that each piece could connect with its companions.

Bach finally decided not merely to present these separate pieces in a simple compositional pattern, but to organise them within an architectural scale. He had long taken account of these factors in the freer forms of concerto, fantasia or prelude; now, they are also subject to fixed forms and cyclical sequences. Such a project might not have seemed possible for a composer of the *basso continuo* age, and, in fact, there is much in Bach's music that does point the way forward to Beethoven. Beethoven would be concerned all his life with questions of the effect of the conclusion and linking of movements, and in his piano sonata Op 110 he 'solved' Bach's 'problem' in his own way: 'sonata form' is 'resolved' in the final fugue.

Perhaps attempts to affirm the universality of the *Art of Fugue* by presenting it as a self-contained cycle are doomed to fail, not because the work is incomplete, but because Bach intended no such thing. Bach had no wish to say 'all' there is to say about a theme through counterpoint, any more than he wanted to accept such a fixed, artificial order. Even if the printing of the *Art of Fugue* were to reflect Bach's ideas, say in the arrangement of numbers one to thirteen, this would offer only one solution. As a whole, perhaps the separate pieces should be regarded as a set of building blocks that can be put together in different ways. The idea that the key to the work lies in its 'correct' arrangement is in danger of obscuring Bach's intentions. Recently, when a source was found showing more clearly than before that the work was intended for keyboard,[140] the practical use of this 'keyboard exercise' was clarified once more.

The *B-minor Mass* revealed Bach's universalism in quite a different sense. Bach probably intended this 'great Catholic Mass', as it is called in the inventory of Carl Philipp Emanuel's estate, as his contribution to ecumenical faith. Whereas he had earlier incorporated the Protestant chorale *O Lamm Gottes unschuldig (O innocent Lamb of*

God) in the opening of the *St Matthew Passion*, he composed the *B-minor Mass*, *Credo in unum deum* (*I believe in One God*) as one of his last *stile antico* movements based on the corresponding intonation of the medieval Mass, which was not unknown in Lutheran worship. This Lutheran who found himself court composer to the Catholic Elector of Protestant Saxony was now making his contribution to the 'one holy Catholic Church', in the broadest sense of the word.

Whether the music existed years before or was new, whether it was original or even 'parody', in the *stile antico* or in the modern 'concerted' manner, in a learned or an entertaining style, the lofty symbolism of the text of the Mass unifies the separate parts without smudging their individuality. Precisely because of Bach's lifelong conern with a diversity of genres, styles and compositional methods, this last work is not uniformly monumental but diversely universal. Thus, he reconciled the years when he was obliged to compose to order with his final wish for a broadly relevant form.

One account of the birth of *Agnus Dei* of the *B-minor Mass* casts light on this. The alto soloist sings: *Lamm Gottes, das der Welt Sünde trägt, erbarm' dich unser* (*O Lamb of God that takest away the sins of the world, have mercy upon us*), a passionate imprecation set to music of unearthly beauty. This appears to be a perfect harmony of text and music. Yet Bach is using an aria from the secular wedding cantata *Auf! süss-entzückende Gewalt* (*Up, sweetly charming power*) BWV Anh I, 14, composed in 1725 to a text by Johann Christoph Gottsched the sense of which runs: 'Begone, begone, all ye cold hearts! Begone, I am your enemy. He who will not give room to love flees happiness and hates his life; to the worst folly he is friend. You choose yourselves a painful end.' As early as 1735, Bach had glossed this aria for the *Ascension Oratorio* BWV 11, with a text consisting of a fervent prayer to heaven-bound Christ: 'Ah stay, ah stay, my dearest life, ah, do not flee from me so soon! If thou must leave, if we must part, 'tis pain and anguish to my heart.'

It was this aria that Bach refashioned for the *Agnus Dei*. In this process, he rejected the operatic *da capo* form as inappropriate to the sacred character of the continuous text but also removed coquettish, sighing figures, giving the voice a soaring melisma before, like its model, it moves into the ritornello theme. This reveals Bach's creative method. The *idea* of an aria, characterised by certain structural and expressive features, existed in his mind long before he wrote it. Bach revealed this 'original' in different versions depending on the time, the choice of text, and the purpose. Thus, he gave concrete forms to ideas that he had previously only imagined.

It is no coincidence that the Romantics, in a time that understood little of the doctrine of affect and figures, the symbolism of keys or numerology, saw Bach's universalism as revelatory. An art-loving layman, the historian Johann Wilhelm Loebell, expressed himself thus to Ludwig Tieck in 1829, reeling from the 'rediscovered' *St Matthew Passion*: 'Sebastian is certainly austere and grave, but in such a way that even amidst the lamentations, grief, repentance and penance, the cheerfulness and the joy of existence still break through in the most wonderful manner, indeed grow directly out of those emotions and flourish. I must tell you that I think I have found in Bach the composer I have sought so long, a musician who may be compared with Shakespeare.'[140]

Epilogue: Bach's place in the history of music

In November 1750, the violin virtuoso and Kappelmeister Johann Georg Pisendel of Dresden, who had many connections with Bach and his work, wrote to Georg Philipp Telemann: 'Three of Mizler's Society have died, Herr Stelzel, Herr Bimler, Herr Bach, and yet I see no mourning ode. *Quare* [why]?'[142]

Telemann needed no more prompting. The following January, Pisendel inserted the following sonnet in the *Neu-eröffnete Historische Correspondenz von Curiosis Saxonicis*:

Sonnet on the late Herr Kapellmeister Bach

Let Italy go on her virtuosi vaunting
Who through the sounding art have there achieved great fame –
On German soil they also will not be found wanting,
Nor can they here be held less worthy of the name.
Departed Bach! Long since thy splendid organ playing
Alone brought thee the noble cognomen 'the Great',
And what thy pen had writ, the highest art displaying,
Did some with joy and some with envy contemplate.

Then sleep! The candle of thy fame ne'er low will burn;
The pupils thou hast trained, and those they train in turn
Prepare thy future crown of glory brightly glowing.
Thy children's hands adorn it with its jewels bright,
But what shall cause thy true worth to be judged aright
Berlin to us now in a worthy son is showing.[143]

The other three great German composers of Bach's time (clockwise from above left): Georg Philipp Telemann, Karl Heinrich Graun and George Frideric Handel. In the view even of his contemporaries, Bach was the equal of any of them. Mezzotint engraving by Valentin Daniel Preissler, 1750; engraving by Valentin Daniel Preissler, 1752; engraving by Johann Georg Wolffgang after Georg Andreas Wolffgang

Johann Sebastian 'the Great' and Carl Philipp Emanuel 'a worthy son' – when Telemann described them in such terms many of his contemporaries must have felt he had hit the nail on the head. By the time he died, Bach *père* was regarded almost as his own memorial throughout Germany, while Carl Philipp Emanuel represented new musical trends in the north German area. A generation earlier Telemann himself had been the trendsetter, the German musician who best represented his time. Telemann, the son of a pastor, had held a highly regarded position as Kantor, like Bach; he was an educator, too, and published didactic works including books of chorales, collections of fugues, and even, in old age, a *Musical Table of Notes and Intervals*, his contribution to a basic theory of music.

But, whereas Bach made use of his authority at Leipzig to concentrate on a high-flown music independent of fashionable trends, Telemann, so far as his position allowed, placed himself entirely at the service of the Enlightenment. His musical style was natural, fluent, melodious, speaking, full of imagery, appealing directly to listeners of every degree of education. Telemann was guided by the aesthetics of folk music, drawing on a variety of ethnic traditions. He had no wish to leave music the sole property of church and court. In a new middle class that was building its own cultural institutions and asserting a particular creative identity, Telemann was a pioneering, savvy entrepreneur working to his own agenda.

Bach hardly stood *in opposition* to this concept of music and musical culture, but more *at a tangent* to it. He could claim all Telemann's qualities and call out, 'Here I am!' The fashionable style? From whom but his own father had Carl Philipp Emanuel learnt the *galant* method? Fluent melody? Look at the *Sanctus* from the *B-minor Mass*. Music for everyone? Consider his audience for the *Coffee Cantata*. An interest in folk music? We have the *Peasant Cantata*. The entrepreneurial promotion of music? From whose mind did the *Klavierübung* spring? Middle-class musical institutions? It was out of Bach's *Collegium Musicum* that the great concert tradition of Leipzig developed.

These are facets only of Bach's complex image, not of his time. The diversity of styles he could employ and the universality of his musical thinking make it impossible to claim him entirely for any one of the great intellectual currents of the time. In writing 24 preludes and fugues in all the keys, Bach embodied the Enlightenment thinker, systematically studying and employing the complete possibilities open to him in his art. The *Klavierübung* project also reflects such 'encyclopaedic' thinking. But when Bach turns to counterpoint, both within and outside the *Klavierübung,* the canon and the fugue, his embodiment of these genres is not so much Enlightened as Faustian: desiring to know what holds the heart of the world together, Bach also stands at the crossroads of medieval alchemy and modern 'scientific' research; like Faust, he had a mind formed by ancient speculative, mystical and pan-sophic traditions, while blazing the trail for a thoroughly modern rationalisation of composition. In so doing he did not give up his individuality. After all, the *Art of Fugue* is fascinating not because Bach presents *all* possibilities of counterpoint, but because he chooses *some* of them to demonstrate his art.

The *Goldberg Variations* futher illuminates these apparent contradictions. While the cycle is as tightly organised as a police state, it is full of puzzles. In the 25th variation adagio, it offers a mood pervaded by melancholy, beyond the rustic humour in the quodlibet based on the popular songs *Ich bin so lang nicht bei dir g'west* and *Kraut und Rüben haben mich vertrieben.* Ultimately, this is an important distinction between Bach on the one hand and Telemann and Handel on the other: Bach was neither an Enlightened entertainer like Telemann, nor a composer like Handel who appealed directly to very human emotions. He cannot be identified with any role or any genre.

Faith, although far from blind, was surely the guiding factor in Bach's life. For him, the *Soli deo gloria* and *Jesu Juva* written above his scores were far more than mere convention. These were the affirmations of a Christian firmly rooted in Lutheranism. Bach had a considerable theological library, and found time not just to read the Bible but to add comments in the margins. The remark of Wilhelm Friedemann Bach concerning Bach and the B – A – C – H note sequence – 'My father was no fool' might be applied to his Piety and Christianity. Independent of any sectarianism, Bach's orthodox Lutheranism, mystical Baroque and Pietistic ideas, and new humanist ideas stemming from the Enlightenment, coexisted.[144]

FAITH

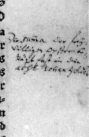

v. 29. Die Webe aber des Erzes war siebenzig Centner / zweytausend und vierhundert Seckel. (nach Agricola Rechnung träget dieses auß 4072 Rthlr. wenn wir nu solche zu der Summa des Goldes und Silbers addiren / kommen zusammen 681339. Rthlr. das macht Meißnischen Gülden 778673. daraus der Segen GOttes und Reichthumb des Volckes abzunemen / daß sie fast in die acht Tonnen Goldes in die Stiffts-Hütten haben schencken können / und noch mehr beygetragen hetten / wenns nicht Moses

The family Bible: marginal comment by Bach on Exodus 38: 29 in his annotated Bible: *The sum of the voluntary offering amounts to almost eight tons of gold.* Bach was noting the value of the temple treasures assembled by the children of Israel for their shrine; he must have read the scriptures with close attention.

However, in certain specific situations, for instance when choosing the texts for his cantatas and *Passions*, Bach may have been swayed by the religious fervour of his particular environments. Weimar, for instance, was more Pietistic than orthodox Leipzig, which only opened up to rationalistic trends towards the end of Bach's life. Yet his own philosophy was not necessarily that of their various messages. Bach always did as he pleased with his models.

The opening words of the *St John Passion*, his impassioned plea to the son of God, completely subsumes the liturgically formulaic diction, *Herr unser Herrscher, dessen Ruhm in allen Landen herrlich ist* (*Lord of lords, whose fame has gone out into all lands*). He is so unaffected by the lyrical opening of such a text as *Gleich wie der Regen und Schnee vom Himmel föllt* (*Like as the rain and snow from heaven do fall*) in BWV 18 that he places the main emphasis on the following litany with its choral refrain *Erhör uns lieber Herre Gott* (*O hearken to us, dear Lord God*). Bach the pan-sophist can scarcely be disentangled from Bach the 'Enlightened' thinker. In his contrapuntal arts does *God* reveal hidden levels of creation through his servant Bach, or is it the *artist* who makes God's creation his own?

Posthumous fame in a pictorial broadsheet: Johann Sebastian and the Bach memorial in Leipzig erected in 1843 on the initiative of Felix Mendelssohn-Bartholdy. Steel engraving by Albert Henry Payne, c.1850

Bach was constantly re-formulating his theological, philosophical, aesthetic and compositional problems, and defies any attempt at classification. He was a 'universalist' only because he was constantly re-creating the world, rather than repeating the 'credo' time and time again. Did this make him 'the last manifestation of the medieval world – the world of Wolfram, the mystics, Dürer and Luther?' Richard Wagner certainly thought so. He compared the language of the *Well-Tempered Clavier* with that of the classic sonata: 'It is like the voice of the thing in itself; the highly-strung and sentimental style seems petty by comparison; in Beethoven everything becomes dramatic.'[145]

And then we also have Bach the dramatist and Bach the sensualist – the modern Bach. Of the making of interpretations there is no end.

der S. Blasii=Kirche, Nahmens, Johann Friedrich, welcher an. 1730 verstorben ist; hat verschiedene feine Clavier= insonderheit aber dergleichen Vocal=Stücke gesetzet, so aber nicht gedruckt worden sind. Ist an. 1703 den 31 Martii, im 60 Jahre seines Alters gestorben. *

Bach (*Joh. Michael*) erstberührten Joh. Christophs zu Eisenach Bruder, gewesener Organist und Stadt=Schreiber zu Gehren, einem Flecken und Amt am Thüringer Walde, Hrn. Johann Sebastian Bachs erster Schwieger=Vater, hat sehr viele Kirchen=Stücke, starcke Sonaten, und Clavier=Sachen gesetzt, wovon aber gleichfalls nichts gedruckt worden ist.

Bach (*Joh. Sebastian*) Hrn. Joh. Ambrosii Bachs, gewesenen Hof= und Raths=Musici zu Eisenach Sohn, gebohren daselbst an. 1685 den 21 Martii, hat bey seinem ältesten Bruder, Hrn. Johann Christoph Bachen, gewesenen Organisten und Schul=Collegen zu Ohrdruff, die ersten Principia auf dem Clavier erlernet, wurde erstl. an. 1703 zu Arnstadt, an der Neuen=Kirche, und an. 1707 zu Mühlhausen an der S. Blasii=Kirche Organist; kam an. 1708 nach Weimar, wurde hieselbst Hochfürstl. Cammer=Musicus und Hof=Organist, an. 1714 Concert=Meister; an. 1717 zu Cöthen Hochfürstl. Capell=Meister, und an. 1723 nach des seel. Hrn. Kuhnauens Tode, Music-Director in Leipzig, auch Hochfürstl. Sachsen=Weißenfelsischer Capell=Meister. Von seinen vortrefflichen Clavier=Sachen sind in Kupffer heraus gekommen: an. 1726 eine Partita aus dem B dur, unter dem Titul: Clavier=Übung, bestehend in Præludien, Allemanden, Couranten, Sarabanden, Giquen, Menuetten, 2c. Dieser ist gefolgt die Zweyte, aus dem C moll; die 3te aus dem A moll; die 4te aus dem D dur; die 5te aus dem G dur, und die 6te aus dem E moll; wormit vermuthlich das Opus sich endiget. Die Bachische Familie soll aus Ungern herstammen, und alle, die diesen Nahmen geführet haben, sollen so viel man weiß, der Music zugethan gewesen seyn; welches vielleicht daher kommt: daß so gar auch die Buchstaben b̄ a c h̄ in ihrer Ordnung melo-

disch sind. (Diese Remarque hat den Leipziger Hrn. Bach zum Erfinder.)

Bacheler (*Daniel*) ein um's Jahr 1610 sehr berühmt gewesener Lautenist in Engelland.

Bachi (*Giov. de*) ein um die Mitte des 16ten seculi bekannt gewesener Componist, von dessen Arbeit in dem von Joh. Montaño und Ulrico Neubero an. 1564 zu Nürnberg edirten Thesauro Musico, T. I. Motetten befindlich sind.

Bachini (*Gislamerio*) hat ein Opus 3.4. - 9 stimmiger Missen ediret. s. *Parstorff.* Catalog. p. 4.

Backhauß, (*Johann*) von Hameln, war unter den 53 Examinatoribus des an. 1596 erbaueten Grüningischen Schloß=Orgelwercks der 2te. s. Werckmeisters Organum Gruningense redivivum, §. 11.

Baconus oder Baco (*Franciscus*) Baro de Verulamio, Vice-Comes S. Albani, Königl. Procurator, Groß=Siegel=Verwahrer, und Cantzler von Engelland, gebohren an. 1560 den 22 Januarii, und gestorben den 9 April. an. 1626. handelt in der gantzen zweyten wie auch größtentheils in der dritten Centuria seiner Historiæ naturalis Sylva Sylvarum genannt, in vier Bogen von physicalischen, nebst andern hauptsächlich auch den Sonum betreffenden Experimentis, unter folgender Überschrifft: Varie hactenus, neque infeliciter, praxis Musicæ exculta est: theoria verò, præcipuè quæ Practicæ caussas continet, admodum perfunctoriè habita: reducta enim est in mysticas quasdam subtilitates, quarum nec vsus nec veritas constat. Itaque pro more nostro contemplativam in activa parte jungemus. Wegen obgedachter geographischer terminorum ist zu mercken: daß Verulam und Fanum Albani einerley, nemlich eine in der Provintz Hardfordshire in Engelland liegende alte Stadt ist; hieselbst liegt er in der S. Michaelis=Kirche begraben. Das aus weisem Marmor bestehende Monument stellet ihn sitzend, als wenn er auf etwas meditire, vor, worunter folgendes Epitaphium, so Henricus Wottonus verfertiget, befindlich ist:

Franciscus Bacon , Baro de Verulam,
S. Albani Vice - Comes:
seu,
Notioribus Titulis,
Scientiarum lumen , Facundiæ Lex

hie

First marks of fame: the entry on Johann Sebastian Bach in Johann Gottfried Walther's *Musicalisches Lexicon* of 1732.

Bach and the Violin

When Bach began studying the violin, he would not have played on one of the Cremonese instruments so beloved of string players today. The Europe-wide vogue for these violins, made by Stradivari, Amatis or Del Gesú, was delayed until long after after their construction, when they were popu-larised by the Italian–French virtuoso, Giovanni Battista Viotti, violinist to Marie Antoinette.

The type of violin Bach played would have been of the model perfected by the Austrian *luthier* Jacob Stainer (*c.*1617–1683). These distinctive, 'high arched' instruments were ideally suited to the highly articulated, 'spoken' musical language of the German Baroque. Indeed, a Stainer violin was listed amongst Bach's effects at death, most likely an inheritance from his father Ambrosius.

The illustration below is of a reconstruction of a Stainer violin made by the leading modern British *luthier*, David Rattray, custodian to the string instrument collection of the Royal Academy of Music, London.

Only two Stainer violins retained their original necks, and Rattray incor-porated dates from these two instruments to create this beautiful example. The 1680 neck type is clearly visible in this side view.

This example is an exciting view of a new violin made in exactly the state that Stainer and, later, Bach would recognise. It is a fine example of the revival of early instrument technology and design made by an important contemporary *luthier* at the peak of his powers.

Notes

There is not enough space in this biography to trace all the paths taken by research and the author's own attitude to them. In the following notes, therefore, the only works cited are those from which literal quotations or the findings of new and still little-known research are taken. The author would like to thank several specialists who have put their lives to the service of Bach scholarship, thus enabling our knowledge to progress beyond mere speculation: Alfred Dürr, Andreas Glöckner, Klaus Hofmann, Dietrich Kilian, Yoshitake Kobayashi, Werner Neumann, Hans-Joachim Schulze, Christoph Wolff.

1 Bach-Dokumente 1, pp. 255ff (for complete title see Further Reading).

2 Hans-Joachim Schulze, 'Bach und Buxtehude', in Bach-Jahrbuch 1991, pp. 177ff.

3 Bach-Dokumente 3, pp. 81f; Engl, Bach Reader, pp. 216f.

4 Bach-Dokumente 3, p. 82; Engl, Bach Reader, p. 217.

5 Gustav Fock, Der junge Bach in Lüneburg (Hamburg 1950), p. 43.

6 Martin Petzoldt, '"Ut probus & doctus reddar." Zum Anteil der Theologie bei der Schulausbildung J. S. Bachs', in Bach-Jahrbuch 1985, pp. 7ff.

7 Bach-Dokumente 3, p. 87; Engl, Bach Reader, p. 223.

8 Bach-Dokumente 3, p. 288; Engl, Bach Reader, p. 278.

9 Bach-Dokumente 2, pp. 19f; Engl, Bach Reader, pp. 51f.

10 Bach-Dokumente 3, p. 82; Engl, Bach Reader, p. 218.

11 Bach-Dokumente 1, p. 19; Engl, Bach Reader, p. 60.

12 Hans-Joachim Schulze, Studien zur Bach-Überlieferung im 18. Jahrhundert (Leipzig and Dresden 1984), pp. 29ff.

13 Christoph Wolff, 'Johann Adam Reinken und J. S. Bach: Zum Kontext des Bachschen Frühwerks', in Bach-Jahrbuch 1985, pp. 99ff.

14 Hermann Keller, Die Orgelwerke Bachs (Leipzig 1948), pp. 64f.

15 J S Bach, Orgelchoräle der Neumeister Sammlung, ed Christoph Wolff (New Haven and Kassel 1985).

16 Bach-Dokumente 3, p. 289 (Engl, Bach Reader, p. 160), and 1, p. 107.

17 Andreas Glöckner, 'Gründe für Johann Sebastian Bachs Weggang von Weimar', in Bericht über die Wissenschaftliche Konferenz zum 5. Internationalen Bachfest in Leipzig 1985 (Leipzig 1988), p. 141.

18 Bach-Dokumente 2, p. 65; Engl, Bach Reader, p. 75.

19 Jean-Claude Zehnder, 'Zu Bachs Stilentwicklung in der Mühlhauser und Weimarer Zeit', in Karl Heller and Hans-Joachim Schulze (eds), Das Frühwerk J. S. Bachs (Cologne 1995), p. 321.

20 Albert Schweitzer, J. S. Bach (Leipzig nd), p. 247.

21 Jörg Demel, Toccata und Präludium in der Orgelmusik von Merulo bis Bach (Kassel etc 1989), pp. 79ff.

22 Schulze, as note 12, pp. 146ff.

23 Werner David, Johann Sebastian Bach's Orgeln (Berlin 1951), p. 88.

24 Erich Reimer, *Die Hofmusik in Deutschland 1500–1800* (Wilhelmshaven 1991), pp. 151ff.

25 Alfred Dürr, *Studien über die frühen Kantaten J. S. Bachs* (2nd edn, Wiesbaden 1977).

26 Hans-Joachim Schulze, 'Telemann – Pisendel – Bach. Zu einem unbekannten Bach-Autograph', in *Die Bedeutung G. Ph. Telemanns für die Entwicklung der europäischen Musikkultur im 18. Jahrhundert*, conference proceedings Magdeburg 1981, Part 2 (Magdeburg 1983), pp. 73ff.

27 Werner Korte, *Musik und Weltbild* (Leipzig 1940).

28 Carl Dahlhaus, 'Bachs konzertante Fugen', in *Bach-Jahrbuch 1955*, pp. 45ff.

29 Werner Breig, 'Bachs Orgelchoral und die italienische Instrumentalemusik', in W Osthoff and R Wiesend (eds), *Bach und die italienische Musik* (Venice 1987), pp. 91f.

30 Heinrich Christoph Koch, *Versuch einer Anleitung zur Composition*, 3 (Leipzig 1793, photomechanical reproduction Hildesheim 1969), pp. 326f.

31 Johann Nikolaus Forkel, *Über Johann Sebastian Bachs Leben, Kunst und Kunstwerke* (Leipzig 1802), p. 58.

32 Anton Webern, *Der Weg zur Neuen Musik*, ed Willi Reich (Vienna 1960), p. 36.

33 For one of the works that are of interest in the context of this chapter, *see* Christian Martin Schmidt, 'Stabilität und Varietät. Zum ersten Satz von Bachs viertem Brandenburgischen Konzert', in Reinmar Emans and Matthias Wendt (eds), *Beiträge zur Geschichte des Konzerts* (Bonn 1990).

34 Heinrich Besseler, *Bach als Wegbereiter*. Reprinted in Walter Blankenburg (ed), *Johann Sebastian Bach.Wege der Forschung*, 170

(Darmstadt 1970), pp. 196ff.

35 Philip Ambrose,'"Weinen, Klagen, Sorgen, Zagen" und die antike Redekunst', in *Bach-Jahrbuch 1980*, pp. 35ff. In general: Arnold Schering, *Das Symbol in der Musik* (Leipzig 1941); Arnold Schmitz, *Die Bildlichkeit der wortgebundenen Musik Johann Sebastian Bachs* (Mainz 1950).

36 Friedrich Smend, *J. S. Bach. Kirchen-Kantaten* (Berlin 1966), series I, pp. 24f.

37 Cosima Wagner, *Die Tagebücher*, 2 (Munich and Zurich 1977), p. 446 and p. 229.

38 Günther Hoppe, 'Köthener politische, ökonomische und höfische Verhältnisse als Schaffensbedingungen Bachs', in *Cöthener Bach-Hefte*, 4 (Köthen 1986), p. 17.

39 Peter Schleuning, 'Der Kapellmeister Bach', in *Programmbuch Bachfest* (Berlin 1989), p. 14. In general: Walther Vetter, *Der Kapellmeister Bach* (Potsdam 1950); Friedrich Smend, *Bach in Köthen* (Berlin 1951).

40 But cf for other opinions Günther Hoppe, 'Köthener Kammerrechnungen – Köthener Hofparteien. Zum Hintergrund der Hofkapellmeisterzeit Johann Sebastian Bachs', in *Bericht*, as note 17, pp. 145ff.

41 Herbet Zimpel, 'Der Streit zwischen Reformierten und Lutheranen in Köthen', in *Bach-Jahrbuch 1979*, pp. 97ff.

42 *Bach-Dokumente 2*, p. 83 and p. 120.

43 *Bach-Dokumente 1*, p. 268.

44 *Bach-Dokumente 3*, p. 285; Engl, *Bach Reader*, p. 277.

45 *Bach-Dokumente 3*, pp. 83f.; Engl, *Bach Reader*, p. 219.

46 *Bach-Dokumente 2*, p. 348; Engl, *Bach Reader*, p. 444.

47 Rudolf Eller, 'Vivaldi – Dresden – Bach', in *Johann Sebastian Bach*, as note 34, pp. 466ff.

48 *Bach-Dokumente 3*, p. 84; Engl, *Bach*

Reader, p. 219.

49   *Bach-Dokumente* 2, pp. 78f.

50   *Bach-Dokumente* 2, pp. 186f; Engl,
      Bach Reader, p. 82.

51   *Bach-Dokumente* 2, p. 219.

52   *Bach-Dokumente* 2, p. 153.

53   Peter Schleuning, 'The Chromatic
      Fantasia of J. S. Bach and the genesis
      of Musical *Sturm und Drang*', in Pieter
      Dirksen (ed), *The Harpsichord and its
      Repertoire*. Proceedings of the
      International Harpsichord
      Symposium (Utrecht 1992).

54   Andreas Glöckner, 'Anmerkungen
      zu Johann Sebastian Bachs Köthener
      Kantatenschaffen', in *Cöthener
      Bach-Hefte*, as note 38, pp. 89ff.

55   Willibald Gurlitt, *J. S. Bach. Der
      Meister und sein Werk* (Berlin 1936; 4th
      edn, Kassel and Basel 1959), p. 62.

56   Martin Geck, 'Gattungstraditionen
      und Altersschichten in den
      Brandenburgischen Konzerten',
      in *Die Musikforschung*, 23 (1970),
      pp. 139ff; Werner Breig, 'Probleme
      der Analyse in Bachs
      Instrumentalkonzerten', in Reinhold
      Brinkmann (ed), *Bachforschung und
      Bachinterpretation heute* (Leipzig 1981),
      pp. 127ff; Christoph Wolff,
      'Probleme und Neuansätze der
      Bach-Biographik', in Reinhold
      Brinkmann (ed), *Bachforschung und
      Bachinterpretation heute* (Leipzig 1981),
      p. 28; Hans-Joachim Schulze,
      'Johann Sebastian Bachs Konzerte –
      Fragen der Überlieferung und
      Chronologie', in Peter Ahnsel et al
      (eds), *Beiträge zum Konzertschaffen
      J. S. Bachs* (Leipzig 1981), pp. 9ff.

57   Peter Schleuning, '"Alle Kreatur
      sehnt sich mit uns und ängstigt sich
      noch immerdar." Fragen des Ersten
      "Brandenburgischen Konzertes" an
      uns', in Hans Werner Henze (ed),
      *Die Chiffren. Musik und Sprache. Neue
      Aspekte der musikalischen Ästhetik*, 4
      (Frankfurt am Main 1990), pp. 219ff.

58   Gerd Rienäcker: 'Beobachtungen
      zur Dramaturgie im ersten Satz

des 5. Brandenburtischen Konzerts',
      in *Beiträge zum Konzertschaffen*, as
      note 56, pp. 63ff.

59   Elmar Budde, 'Musikalische Form
      und rhetorische disposition im
      ersten Satz des dritten
      Brandenburgischen Konzerts von
      J. S. Bach', in *Beiträge zum
      Konzertschaffen*, as note 56, pp. 63ff.

60   Hans Eppstein, *Studien über J. S. Bachs
      Sonaten für ein Melodieinstrument und
      obligates Cembalo* (Uppsala 1966);
      Hans Vogt, *Johann Sebastian Bachs
      Kammermusik* (Stuttgart 1981).

61   Forkel, as note 31, p. 31.

62   Georg Feder, 'Geschichte der
      Bearbeitungen von Bachs
      Chaconne', in Martin Geck (ed),
      Bach-Interpretationen (Göttingen
      1969), p. 180.

63   Hans Heinrich Eggebrecht, *Bachs
      Kunst der Fuge. Erscheinung und
      Deutung* (Munich and Zurich 1984);
      Ursula Kirkendale, 'The Source for
      Bach's Musical Offering: The
      Institutio Oratoria of Quintilian', in
      *Journal of the American Musicological
      Society*, 33 (1980), pp. 88ff.

64   *Bach-Dokumente* 2, p. 92; Engl, *Bach
      Reader*, p. 88.

65   *Bach-Dokumente* 1, p. 67; Engl, *Bach
      Reader*, p. 125.

66   On the problem as a whole, see
      Hans-Joachim Schulze, '". . . da man
      nun die besten nicht bekommen
      könne . . .". Kontroversen und
      Kompromisse vor Bachs Leipziger
      Amtsantritt', in *Bericht über die
      Wissenschaftliche Konferenz zum 3.
      Internationalen Bachfest der DDR 1975*
      (Leipzig 1977), pp. 71ff; Ulrich
      Siegele, 'Bachs Stellung in der
      Leipziger Kulturpolitik seiner Zeit',
      in *Bach-Jahrbücher* 1983, 1984, 1986.

67   *Grosses vollständiges Universal Lexicon*,
      16 (Halle and Leipzig 1737), col 180of.

68   Arnold Schering, *Musikgeschichte
      Leipzigs*, 2 (Leipzig 1826), p. 206.

69   Andreas Glöckner, 'Johann Kuhnau,
      J. S. Bach und die Musikdirektoren

der Leipziger Neukirche', in *Beiträge zur Bachforschung*, 4 (Leipzig 1985), p. 29; Andreas Glöckner, *Die Musikpflege an der Leipziger Neukirche zur Zeit Johann Sebastian Bachs* (Leipzig 1990).

70 *Stadtarchiv Leipzig*, Urkundensammlung 97, 1, kindly made available by Dr Andreas Glöckner.

71 *Bach-Dokumente* 2, pp. 94 and 96, and 1, p. 177; Engl, *Bach Reader*, p. 92.

72 *Bach-Dokumente* 2, p. 184.

73 *Bach-Dokumente* 2, p. 104.

74 *Bach-Dokumente* 2, p. 104; Engl, *Bach Reader*, p. 93.

75 Günther Stiller, *Johann Sebastian be und das Leipziger gottesdienstliche Leben seiner Zeit* (Berlin 1970).

76 Susan Gilmour Bailey, 'An intimacy between strangers: Reflections on performance of composition from the *Notenbüchlein für Anna Magdalena Bach*' Royal Academy of Music, MMus 17/09/2001.

77 *Bach-Dokumente* 2, p. 205; Engl, *Bach Reader*, p. 120.

78 *Bach-Dokumente* 1, pp. 60ff; Engl, *Bach Reader*, pp. 121f.

79 *Bach-Dokumente* 1, pp. 67f; Engl, *Bach Reader*, p. 125.

80 Alfred Dürr, *Zur Chronologie der Leipziger Vokalwerke J. S. Bach* (2nd edn, Kassel etc 1976); Georg von Dadelsen, *Beiträge zur Chronologie der Werke Johann Sebastian Bachs* (Trossingen 1958); Wolf Hobohn, 'Neue "Texte zur Leipziger Kirchen-Music"', in *Bach-Jahrbuch* 1973, pp. 5ff.

81 Andreas Glöckner, 'Überlegungen zu J. S. Bachs Kantatenschaffen nach 1730', in *Beiträge zur Bachforschung*, 6 (Leipzig 1988), pp. 54ff.

82 Martin Geck, *Johann Sebastian Bach. Johannespassion* (Munich 1991), pp. 21ff.

83 Martin Geck, *Die Wiedeerentdeckung der Matthäuspassion im 19. Jahhundert. Die zeitgenössischen Dukumente und ihre ideengeschichtliche Deutung* (Regensburg 1967), pp. 16 and 46.

84 Stiller, as note 75, pp. 44–6.

85 *Bach-Dokumente* 2, pp. 234f; Werner Neumann, 'Das "Bachische Collegium Musicum"', in *Bach-Jahrbuch* 1960, pp. 5ff.

86 *Bach-Dokumente* 3, p. 241.

87 Hans-Joachim Schulze, 'J. S. Bachs Missa H-Moll. Die Dresdner Widmungsstimmen von 1733', in Ulrich Prinz (ed), *J. S. Bach. Messe H-Moll* (Stuttgart and Kassel 1990), pp. 84ff.

88 *Bach-Dokumente* 2, pp. 277–80.

89 Hans-Joachim Kreutzer, 'Bach und das literarische Leipzig', in *Bach-Jahrbuch* 1991, p. 21.

90 *Bach-Dokumente* 2, p. 250; Engl, *Bach Reader*, p. 158.

91 *Bach-Dokumente* 2, p. 278.

92 Peter Schleuning, *Das 18. Jahrhundert: Der Bürger erhebt sich* (Reinbek 1984), pp. 115ff; Hans-Werner Heister, *Das Konzert. Theorie einer Kulturform*, 2 vols (Wilhelmshaven 1983).

93 Andreas Glöckner, 'Neuerkenntnisse zu J. S. Bachs Aufführunskalender zwischen 1729 und 1735', in *Bach-Jahrbuch* 1981, pp. 43ff.

94 *Bach-Dokumente* 1, p. 139.

95 Werner Breig, 'J. S. Bach und die Entstehung des Klavierkonzerts', in *Archiv für Musikwissenschaft*, year 36 (1979), pp. 21ff.

96 Christian Berger, 'J. S. Bachs Klavierkonzerte', in *Archiv für Musikwissenschaft*, year 47 (1990), pp. 207ff.

97 Martin Geck, 'Spuren eines Enzelgängers. Die "Bauernkantata" oder: vom unergründlichen Humor der Picander und Bach', in *Neue Zeitschrift für Musik*, year 135 (1992), pp. 24ff.

98 *Bach-Dokumente* 2, pp. 160f.

99 Werner Neumann, 'Einige neue Quellen zu J. S. Bachs Herausgabe eigener und zum Mitvertrieb fremder Werke', in *Musica – Mens –*

Musici. Gedenkschrift für Walther Vetter (Leipzig 1969), p. 166.

100 *Bach-Dokumente* 2, p. 223.

101 Schulze, as note 12, pp. 96ff.

102 Hans-Joachim Schulze, 'Bemerkungen zur Leipziger Literaturszene. Bach und seine Stellung zur schönen Literatur', in *Bach-Studien*, 7 (Leipzig 1982), p. 162.

103 *Allgemeine Deutsche Biographie*, 26 (Leipzig 1888), p. 398.

104 *Bach-Dokumente* 1, p. 111; 2, pp. 217, 325, 371, 384 and p. 391f.

105 *Bach-Dokumente* 1, pp. 119f; Engl, *Bach Reader*, p. 183.

106 *Bach-Dokumente* 2, p. 373; Engl, *Bach Reader*, p. 234.

107 *Bach-Dokumente* 2, p. 335.

108 Friedrich Smend, *J. S. Bach bei seinem namen gerufen* (Kassel and Basel 1950; reprinted in *Bach-Studien* 1969).

109 For instance: Ludwig Prautzsch, *Vor deinen Thron tret ich hiermit. Figuren und Symbole in den letzten Werken J. S. Bachs* (Neuhausen-Stuttgart 1980); Hertha Kluge-Kahn, *J. S. Bach. Die verschlüsselten theologischen Aussagen in seinem Spätwerk* (Wolfenbüttel and Zurich 1985).

110 Ruth Tatlow, *Bach and the Riddle of the Number Alphabet* (Cambridge 1991).

111 Philipp Spitta, *J. S. Bach*, 2 (Wiesbaden 1964), p. 685.

112 Spitta, as note 110, p. 263.

113 *Bach-Dokumente* 2, p. 336; Engl, *Bach Reader*, p. 249.

114 Forkel, as note 31, p. 48.

115 Hans Joachim Marx, 'Bach und der "Theatralische Stil"', in Christoph Wolff (ed), *Johann Sebastian Bachs Spätwerk und dessen Umfeld* (Kassel etc 1988), pp. 148ff.

116 Ludwig Finscher, 'Zum Parodieproglem bei Bach', in Geck, as note 62, p. 105.

117 Christoph Wolff, 'Zur musikalischen Vorgeschichte des Kyrie aus J. S. Bachs Mess in H-moll', in *Festschrift für Bruno Stäblein* (Kassel etc 1967), pp. 316ff.

118 *Bach-Dokumente* 2, p. 286; Engl, *Bach Reader*, p. 238.

119 *Bach-Dokumente* 2, p. 371.

120 Johann Mattheson, *Der vollkommenen Capellmeister*, facsimile reprint (Kassel etc 1987), p. 441.

121 Rolf Dammann, accompanying text to complete edition of the *Art of Fugue* (1962).

122 *Bach-Dokumente* 2, pp. 434f; Engl, *Bach Reader*, p. 176.

123 Yoshitake Kobayashi, 'Die Universalität in Bachs h-moll-Messe. Ein Beitrag zum Bach-Bild der letzten Lebensjahre', in *Musik und Kirche*, 57 (1987), pp. 9ff.

124 Christine Fröde, 'Zu einer Kritik des Thomanerchores von 1749', in *Bach-Jahrbuch* 1984, pp. 57f.

125 Fröde, as note 123, p. 53.

126 Christoph Wolff, 'Probleme und Neuansätze der Bach-Biographik', in *Bachforschung und Bachinterpretation*, as note 56, p. 29.

127 *Bach-Dokumente* 2, p. 462.

128 *Bach-Dokumente* 3, p. 85; Engl, *Bach Reader*, p. 220.

129 Eike Rauchfuss and Thomas Vieth, 'Betrachtungen über einen möglichen Zusammenhang zwischen Augenoperationen und Todesursache bei J. S. Bach', in *Bach-Jahrbuch* 1989, pp. 221ff; Detlev Kranemann, 'J. S. Bachs Krankheit und Todesursache. Versuch einer Deutungt' in *Bach-Jahrbuch* 1990, pp. 53ff.

130 Christoph Wolff, 'Johann Sebastian Bachs "Sterbechoral": Kritische Fragen zu einem Mythos'; Engl, 'The Deathbed Chorale: Exploding a Myth', in *Studies in Renaissance and Baroque Music in Honor of Arthur Mendel* (Kassel 1974), pp. 283ff.

131 Christoph Trautmann, '"Calovii Schrifften. 3. Bände" aus J. S. Bachs Nachlass und ihre Bedeutung für das Bild des lutherischen Kantors Bach', reprinted from *Musik und Kirche*, 4 (1969).

132 *Bach-Dokumente* 2, p. 274; Engl, *Bach Reader*, p. 188.

133 *Ludwig van Beethovens sämtliche Briefe*, ed. Emerich Kastner, 2nd edn, revised by Julius Kapp (Leipzig 1923), p 41.

134 Berlin and Königsberg 1774, pp. 156f; Engl, *Bach Reader*, p. 260.

135 Willem Elders, 'Kompositionsverfahren in der Musik der alten Niederländer und die Kunst J. S. Bachs', in *Beiträge zur Bachforschung*, 6 (Leipzig 1988), pp. 110ff.

136 Rolf Dammann, *J. S. Bach 'Goldberg-Variationen'* (Mainz 1986), pp. 246ff.

137 *Bach-Dokumente* 2, p. 349.

138 Peter Schleuning, *Die Kunst der Fuge. Ideologien – Entstehung – Analyse* (Kassel and Basle 1993). Eggebrecht, as note 63.

139 Nicole Schwindt-Gross, *Drama und Diskurs. Zur Beziehung zwischen Satztechnik und motivischem Prozess am Beispiel der durchbrochenen Arbeit in den Streichquartetten Mozarts und Haydns* (Laaber 1989).

140 Cf Thomas Wilhelmi's contribution to the *Bach-Jahrbuch* 1992.

141 Geck, as note 82, p. 36.

142 *Bach-Dokumente* 2, p. 513.

143 *Bach-Dokumente* 3, pp. 6f; Engl, *Bach Reader*, p. 227.

144 Martin Petzoldt, 'Zwischen Orthodoxie, Pietismus und Aufklärung – Überlegungen zum theologiegeschichtlichen Kontext J. S. Bachs', in *Bach-Studien*, 7, as note 101, pp. 66ff.

145 Cosima Wagner, as note 37, pp. 227 and 315.

Chronology

Year	History	Culture
1685	In France, Louis XIV revokes Edict of Nantes. In England, Charles II dies; James II becomes king (until 1688). In England, Duke of Monmouth's rebellion. K'ang-hsi opens all Chinese ports to trade.	
1694	The Bank of England is founded.	Rudolf Camerarius, *De sexu plantarum epistola.*
1695	In England, government press censorship ended. Nehemiah Grew isolates magnesium sulphate (Epsom salts) from spring water.	Henry Purcell, *The Indian Queen* and *The Tempest.* William Congreve, *Love for Love.*
1699	In Russia, Peter the Great conquers Azov and Kamchatka.	François de Salignac de la Mothe Fénelon, *Télémaque.*
1700	In Spain, Charles II (Habsburg) dies childless; Philip V (Bourbon) becomes king (until 1746). Great Northern War (until 1721). Administrative reorganisation of Bengal under Sir Charles Eyre. Berlin Academy of Science is founded.	Congreve, *The Way of the World.*
1702	In England, William III dies; Anne becomes queen (until 1714). Britain, Holland and Austria-Hungary declare war against France. The Asiento Company is founded to control slave trade to Spanish America.	Daniel Defoe, *The Shortest Way with Dissenters.* Edward Hyde, *The History of the Rebellion. The Daily Courant,* first daily newspaper published.
1703	Methuen Treaty: Portugal joins Grand Alliance. In Japan, the Chushingura Incident: Kiva Yoshinaka murdered by supporters of Lord of Ako. In Spain, Archduke Charles proclaimed king. In Russia, Peter the Great lays foundations of St Petersburg. Delaware becomes a separate colony from Pennsylvania.	Sébastien de Brossard writes first dictionary of music.

Year	Age	Life
1705	20	At the end of the year, Bach goes on a journey of three or four months to visit Dietrich Buxtehude in Lübeck.
1707	22	On 15 June, Bach is appointed organist of the church of St Blasius in Mühlhausen. On 17 October, he marries his second cousin Maria Barbara Bach in Dornheim.
1708	23	In June, Bach is appointed organist and chamber musician to Dukes Wilhelm Ernst and Ernst August of Weimar. His daughter Catharina Dorothea is born on 29 December.
1710	25	Bach's son Wilhelm Friedemann is born on 22 November.
1713	28	In December, Bach applies for the post of organist at the church of Our Lady in Halle, but withdraws his application in February 1714.
1714	28	On 2 March, Bach is appointed *Konzertmeister* in Weimar. His son Carl Philipp Emanuel is born on 8 March.
1715	30	Bach's son Johann Gottfried Bernhard is born on 11 May.

Year	History	Culture
1705	In Austria-Hungary, Leopold I dies; Joseph I becomes emperor. In Tunis, Husseinite dynasty of Beys overthrows Turks.	G F Handel, *Almira*. Prosper Jolyot Crébillon, *Idoménée*. John Vanbrugh, *The Confederacy*.
1707	In India, Moghul emperor Aurangzeb dies; Bahadur becomes emperor. Act of Union between England and Scotland. Perpetual Alliance signed between Prussia and Sweden. In England, John Floyer introduces the practice of counting the rate of pulse-beats of patients.	George Farquhar, *The Beaux' Strategem*. Gottfried Silbermann builds first organ.
1708	In Brazil, war of Emboabas between Portuguese and Paulistas. In Holland, Jesuits expelled. First accurate map made of China.	Jean-François Regnard, *La Légitaire universel*.
1709	First Russian prisoners sent to Siberia. In Russia, the Great Plague. Rising of Afghans at Kandahar under Mir Vais. Battle of Poltava: Swedish hegemony in the Baltic ends.	Bartolomeo Cristofori builds the first pianoforte. William Byrd, *The Secret Diary of W B Westover*.
1713	Treaty of Utrecht: Philip V, a Bourbon, recognised as king of Spain; Spain and France are never to be united under one king; France cedes Nova Scotia, Newfoundland, Hudson's Bay and St Kitts to Britain. In Prussia, Frederick I dies; Frederick William I becomes elector (until 1740). Charles XII of Sweden taken prisoner by Turkish Sultan (until 1714).	Joseph Addison, *Cato*. Scipione Maffei, *Merope*. In London, Alexander Pope, Jonathan Swift, William Congreve and others found the Scriblerus Club. Abbé Saint Pierre, *Projet pour la Paix Perpétuelle*. In France, the School of Dance is established at the Paris Opéra.
1714	Peter the Great conquers Finland. In Britain, Anne dies; George I becomes king of England and Scotland (until 1727). In India, Moghals defeat rebellion of Sikhs under Banda Bahadur. Daniel Fahrenheit invents mercury thermometer.	Gottfried Wilhelm von Leibnez, *Mondalogie*.
1715	In France, Louis XIV dies; Louis XV becomes king of France (until 1774), under regency of Duc d'Orléans (until 1723). In England and Scotland, Jacobite rebellion suppressed. In South Carolina, rising of Yamassees and other native Indian groups.	Alain-René Lesage, *Gil Blas de Santillane*. Giovanni Tiepolo, *Sacrifice of Isaac*.

Year	Age	Life
1717	32	Bach is appointed court Kapellmeister to Prince Leopold of Anhalt-Köthen in Köthen. In the autumn he goes to Dresden, where, according to tradition, a musical competition with the French keyboard virtuoso Louis Marchand is supposed to take place (Marchand refuses to participate. From 6 November to 2 December, Bach is imprisoned at the court of Weimar because of his request to leave his post there. He is subsequently dishonourably dismissed.
1720	35	Maria Barbara Bach is buried on 7 July. In November, Bach goes to Hamburg, and as a result of his visit applies for the post of organist at the church of St Jacobi, but leaves again before the official auditions.
1721	36	On 3 December, Bach is married to Anna Magdalena Wilcke, chamber singer and daughter of the court trumpeter of Weissenfels.
1722	37	In December, Bach applies for the position of Kantor of St Thomas's in Leipzig.
1723	37–8	On 7 February, Bach auditions in Leipzig; on 5 May, he signs the contract for the post; he moves to Leipzig on 22 May, and performs his inaugural music at St Thomas's church on 30 May.
1724	38–9	His son Gottfried Heinrich is born on 26 February. The first performance of the *St John Passion* takes place in the church of St Nikolai on 7 April.
1725	40	In November, Bach goes to Dresden to give organ recitals.
1726	41–2	Bach's daughter Elisabeth Juliana Friederica is baptised on 5 April. The first performance of the *St Matthew Passion* probably takes place in the church of St Thomas's on 11 April.
1728	43	Bach's daughter Regina Johanna is baptised on 10 October.

Year	History	Culture
1717	In North America, Shenandoah Valley settled by Europeans; native Indians evicted.	Handel, *Water Music*. Antoine Watteau, *Embarkation for the Isle of Cytheria*.
1720	Spain occupies Texas. 'South Sea Bubble' crisis: major financial collapse and political crisis in Britain.	In London, first opera season at Royal Academy. Bernard de Montfaucon, *L'Antiquité Expliqué*.
1721	Clement XI dies; Innocent XIII becomes pope. In Britain, Robert Walpole becomes first lord of the treasury. China suppresses revolution in Formosa.	Handel, *Acis and Galatea*.
1722	In China, accession of Shih Tsung; beginning of Yung Cheng dynasty. Charles VI founds the Dutch East India Company. Peter the Great conquers Baku: gains access to the Black Sea.	Jean-Philippe Rameau, *Traité de l'harmonie*. Defoe, *Moll Flanders*. Richard Steele, *The Conscious Lovers*.
1723	In France, Louis XV attains his majority. Turkey attacks Persia.	Rameau, *L'Endriague*. Voltaire, *La Ligue* (renamed *La Henriade*, 1728).
1724	Afghan ruler Mahmud becomes insane and orders the massacre of Persian nobility and royal family. In Spain, Philip V abdicates. Treaty of Constantinople: Russia and Turkey divide Persia. In Paris, Bourse opens.	Jonathan Swift, *Drapier's Letters*. Melchor Perez Holguin, *The Four Evangelists*.
1725	In Russia, death of Peter the Great; Catherine I becomes tsarina. Congress of Cambrai breaks up Treaty of Vienna.	Joseph Fux, *Gradus ad Parnassum*. Giambattista Vico, *Scienza nuova intorno alla natura*.
1726	In France, Cardinal Fleury is chief minister (until 1743). Voltaire liberated from Bastille; goes to England (until 1728).	Rameau, *Nouveau système de musique théorique*. Swift, *Gulliver's Travels*.
1728	Convention of the Pardo. Vitus Bering discovers straits which separate north-east Asia from north-west America.	John Gay, *The Beggars' Opera*. Alexander Pope, *The Dunciad*.

Year	Age	Life
1729	43–4	Wilhelm Friedemann is registered at Leipzig University on 5 March. Bach becomes director of a *Collegium Musicum* in the spring.
1730	45	There are complaints that Bach is neglecting his duties at the school in the summer. On 23 August, Bach himself complains to the city council about the poor organisation of church music in Leipzig. On 28 October, he expresses great dissatisfaction with his present situation in a letter to Georg Erdmann, his childhood friend.
1731	46	In September, Bach gives organ recitals in Dresden.
1732	47	Bach's son Johann Christoph Friedrich (the 'Bückeburg Bach') is born on 21 June.
1733	48	Wilhelm Friedemann is appointed organist of St Sophia's in Dresden on 23 June. In July, Bach travels to the court of Dresden to present the *Kyrie* and *Gloria* of what would later be the *B-minor Mass*.
1734	49	The first performance of the *Christmas Oratorio* takes place at the end of 1734, beginning of 1735.
1735	50	Bach's son Johann Christian is born on 5 September.
1736	51	The 'dispute of the prefects' begins in July. On 19 November, Bach is appointed court composer to the Electorate of Saxony.
1737	52	In spring, Bach resigns as director of the *Collegium Musicum*.
1738	53	Carl Philipp Emanuel Bach becomes harpsichordist to the Crown Prince of Prussia, later King Friedrich II (Frederick the Great).

Year	History	Culture
1729	North and South Carolina become British colonies. In North America, English found Baltimore. In east Africa, Muscat Arabs take Mombassa from Portugal. In China, Emperor Yung Cheng prohibits opium smoking.	Swift, *A Modest Proposal*. James and Benjamin Franklin, *The Pennsylvania Gazette*. In Constantinople, publication of secular Turkish works begins.
1730	Benedict XIII dies; Clement XII becomes pope (until 1740). In Russia, Peter II dies; Anna becomes tsarina.	Johann Adolph Hasse, *Artaserse*. Johann Christoph Gottsched, *Kritische Dichtkunst*. William Hogarth begins his sequence of narrative pictures.
1731	Second Treaty of Vienna.	Pierre Carlet de Chamblain de Marivaux, *La Vie de Marianne*.
1732	Protestants driven from Salzburg take refuge in Prussia.	J B S Chardin, *Kitchen table with shoulder of mutton*.
1733	War of Polish Succession (until 1738). In Britain, Excise Crisis. In North America, James Oglethorpe founds Georgia.	Rameau, *Hippolytus and Aricio*. Pope, *Essay on Man*. Antoine François Prévost, *Manon Lescaut*.
1734	Turkish-Persian war (until 1735). In Ceylon, rebellion against Dutch.	Voltaire, *Lettres philosophiques*.
1735	In China, Chien Lung becomes emperor.	Rameau, *Les Indes galantes*.
1736	In Poland, Stanislaus I formally abdicates. In Persia, Nadir Shah deposes Safavid dynasty. In Britain, statutes against witchcraft are repealed. Pope Clement XII condemns freemasonry. Leonhard Euler founds the study of mechanics based on differential equations.	Giovanni Battista Pergolesi, *Stabat Mater*.
1737	Grand duke of Tuscany dies; last of the Medicis. In North America, William Byrd founds Richmond, Virginia.	Chardin, *The Draughtsman*.
1738	Third Treaty of Vienna. In Britain, John Wesley begins Methodist revival.	Handel, *Israel in Egypt* and *Saul*.

Year	Age	Life
1739	54	The 'misguided son', Johann Gottfried Bernhard, dies on 27 May. In October, Bach resumes his activities with the *Collegium Musicum*.
1742	56	Bach's daugher Regina Susanna is baptised on 22 February.
1746	61	Wilhelm Friedemann is appointed organist at the church of Our Lady in Halle.
1747	62	Bach visits Friedrich II and the court in Potsdam on 7–8 May, and improvises on the theme of what would become the *Musical Offering*. In June, he joins the 'Corresponding Society of the Musical Sciences' founded by Lorenz Mizler.
1750	64–5	In January, Johann Christoph Friedrich Bach is appointed court musician in Bückeburg. At the end of March and beginning of April Bach undergoes two eye operations. He dies on 28 July, and is buried in St John's cemetery on 30 or 31 July.

Year	History	Culture
1739	War of Jenkins' Ear between Britain and Spain. In west Africa, Yorumba kingdom of Oyo conquers Dahomey. Peace of Belgrade: Austria-Hungary cedes Orsova, Belgrade and Serbia to Turkey.	Francisco Antonio d'Almeida, *La Spinalba*. David Hume, *A Treatise on Human Nature*. Bernard de Montfaucon compiles *Bibliotheca Bibliothecarum*.
1742	In India, Joseph-François Dupleix becomes governor-general of French possessions. Treaty of Berlin. Anders Celsius invents centigrade (or Celsius) temperature scale.	Handel, *Messiah*. Henry Fielding, *Joseph Andrews*. Edward Young, *The Complaint, or Night Thoughts on Life, Death and Immortality*.
1746	In Spain, Philip V dies; Ferdinand VI becomes king. In Scotland, Battle of Culloden: final defeat of Jacobites. In India, French conquer Madras. In China, persecution of Christians.	Etiénne Bonnot and Abbé Condillac, *Essai sur l'origine des connaissances humaines*. Albert von Haller, *Disputationes Anatomicae Selectiones*.
1747	Britain win naval battle of Belle-Isle. Nadir Shah assassinated; Ahmad Khan Abdali founds kingdom of Afghanistan.	William Collins, *Odes*. Thomas Gray, *Ode on Eton College*. Benjamin Franklin, *Plain Truth*.
1750	In Portugal, Pombal becomes chief minister. In Europe, tea becomes fashionable drink.	John Cleland, *The Memoirs of a Woman of Pleasure*. Frederick the Great, *Oeuvres du Philosophe de Sanssouci*. Jean-Jacques Rousseau, *Discours sur les arts et les sciences*.

Select Discography

CONCERTOS

Brandenburg Concertos Nos. 1–6, BWV 1046–51. Teldec 4509 98442-2.
Il Giardino Armonico

KEYBOARD CONCERTOS

Complete solo and multiple concertos. DG ADD/ Dig. 463 725-2. English
Concert, Pinnock (cond. & harpsichord)

KEYBOARD MUSIC

Chromatic Fantasia & Fugue, BWV 903; English Suites nos. 1–6, BWV
802–5; Goldberg Variations BWV 988: 2 & 3-Part Inventions, BWV
772a–786, French Suites Nos. 1–6, BWV 812–17; Partitas Nos. 1–6, BWV
825–30; Well-Tempered Clavier, Books I–II, Preludes & Fugues Nos 1–48,
BWV 646–93. Decca 452 279-2. Schiff (piano)

Goldberg Variations, BWV 988; Well-Tempered Clavier: Fugues in E,
BWV 878 & F sharp min., BWV 902. Sony mono SMK 52594 (1955
recording). Gould (piano)

THE ART OF FUGUE, BWV 1080

CDA 67138. Delmé Quartet, Hyp. CDA 67138

HM HMX 2908084. Moroney (modern harpsichord)

CELLO SUITES, BWV 1002–17

EMI mono CHS7 61027-2. Casals

FLUTE SONATAS, BWV 1030–35

CRD 3314/5. Preston (flute) with Pinnock and Savall (continuo)

VIOLIN

Violin Sonatas Nos. 1–3, BWV 1001, 1003 & 1005 (unaccompanied); Violin
Partitas Nos. 1–3, BWV 1002, 1004 & 1006

Channel CCS 12198 & 14498. Podger (period instrument)

Sony mono MP2K 46721. Szeryng (violin)

Sonatas for violin & harpsichord Nos. 1–6 BWV 1014–19, Sonatas for Violin and Continuo, BWV 1021, 1023 & 1024. Manze (violin) with Egarr, Ter Linden (continuo)

Double Violin Concertos, BWV 1041–3. EMI mono CDH5 67201-2. Menuhin (violin) with Enuscu (violin), Monteux (cond)

ORGAN MUSIC

Tom Koopman Complete Teldec Series Vol. 1–10

Koopman (organ) Teldec

CANTATAS

Complete Cantatas: BIS Masaaki Suzuki Series with Japan Bach Collegium. Suzuki (cond.) BIS

CHORAL WORKS

Christmas Oratorio, BWV 248. DG 423 232-2. Gardiner (cond) Monteverdi Choir with Johnson, Argenta, Von Otter, Blochwitz, Baer.

Magnificat in D, BWV 243 Chan. 0518. Coll. Mus., Hickox (cond) with Kirkby, Bonner, Chance, Ainsley, Varcoe

Mass in B min. BWV 232. H.H. HMX 2908110.2 Herreweghe (cond) with Zorner, Gens, Scholl, Prégardien, Kooy

St John Passion, BWV 245 (sung in English). Double Decca 443 859-2. Britten (cond), Wandsworth School Boys' Choir, ECO, with Pears, Harper, Hodgson, Tear, Howell, Shirley-Quirk.

St Matthew Passion, BWV 244. Teldec 8573 81036-2. Harnoncourt (cond), VCM, Schoenberg Choir, with Fink, Magnus, Röschmann, Schäfer, Goerne, Henschel, Prégardien, Schade, M. Schäfer, Widmer

Further Reading

EDITIONS OF THE WORKS AND DOCUMENTS

Johann Sebastian Bachs Werke, ed by the Leipzig Bachgesellschaft, published over 48 years (Leipzig 1851–99): the first great complete edition in musical history, soon followed by similar editions of the works of Handel and of Palestrina. An impressive achievement for its time, compiled with the support of Brahms and others.

Johann Sebastian Bach, new edition of the complete works, ed by the Johann-Sebastian-Bach-Institut of Göttingen and the Bach-Archiv of Leipzig (Kassel etc 1954 onwards): this edition approaches perfection. With the critical notes separately appended to each volume of musical notation, it offers the essential basis for any serious study of Bach. Study editions of many of the volumes of this edition are available in a smaller format.

J. S. Bach. Sämtliche Kantatentexte, ed Werner Neumann (Leipzig 1956): an invaluable edition of the texts of all the cantatas, although it now needs revision.

Bach-Dokumente, ed by the Bach-Archiv of Leipzig (Kassel and Leipzig 1963–72): volume I contains documents written by J S Bach himself; volume II contains manuscripts and printed documents relating to his life from 1685 to 1750 by other people; volume III contains documents on the later influence of J S Bach 1750–1800. Exhaustive source material, the basis for any biography. A single-volume paperback edition is available as: *J. S. Bach. Leben und Werk in Dokumenten* (Kassel and Leipzig 1975).

Bilddokumente zur Lebensgeschichte J. S. Bachs, ed Werner Neumann (Kassel and Leipzig 1979): a major pictorial documentation of portraits that have come down to us under Bach's name (although their authenticity has not been adequately discussed), with pictures of places connected with Bach's life, Bach manuscripts and printed works, as well as portraits of people who moved in Bach's circle.

CATALOGUES, BIBLIOGRAPHIES, COMPENDIA, ETC.

Bach-Bibliographie, reprint of the catalogues of writings on J S Bach (*Bach-Jahrbuch* 1905–1984), with a supplement and index, ed Christoph Wolff (Berlin 1985): a temporary substitute for a comprehensive Bach bibliography.

Bach Compendium: analytical and biographical repertory of the works of J S Bach, ed Hans-Joachim Schulze and Christoph Wolff (Leipzig 1986 onwards). So far, volume I in four parts, comprising the complete vocal works of Bach, has been published. In the future this compendium, edited with the utmost care, will be *the* catalogue of Bach's works. It contains the opening music of the various works, information on the musical forces involved, the texts, the history of the works, the sources, editions and literature on the subject.

Thematisch-systematisches Verzeichnis der musikalischen Werke von J. S. Bach, ed Wolfgang Schmieder (2nd edn, Wiesbaden 1990) (= Bach-Werke-Verzeichnis, BWV).

Bach-Werke-Verzeichnis. Kleine Ausgabe, ed Alfred Dürr and Yoshitake Kobayashi (Wiesbaden 1998) (= Bach-Werke-Verzeichnis BWV2a): this edition of the catalogue reflects the latest state of research.

YEARBOOKS, COLLECTED VOLUMES, CONCERT GUIDES, REFERENCE WORKS

Bach-Jahrbuch, ed by the Neue Bachgesellschaft, Leipzig (later Berlin, recently Leipzig again), continuously since 1904: the contributions reflect the latest scholarship at the respective times of the yearbooks' publication, especially in the biographical area.

Hans Vogt, *Johann Sebastian Bachs Kammermusik. Voraussetzungen, Analysen, Einzelwerke* (Stuttgart 1981).

Konzertführer Johann Sebastian Bach (Leipzig and Mainz 1984): in general, good introductions to selected vocal works and Bach's orchestral, chamber and keyboard music.

Alfred Dürr, *Die Kantaten von J. S. Bach*, 2 vols (2nd edn, Kassel and Munich 1985): the specialist reference work for the cantatas, containing all the texts.

Die Welt der Bachkantaten, ed Christoph Wolff and Ton Koopman, 1–3 (Stuttgart and Kassel 1996). English edition 1997.

Bach und die Nachwelt, ed Michael Heinemann and Hans-Joachim Hinrichsen, four vols to date (Laaber 1997 onwards).

Peter Williams, *J. S. Bachs Orgelwerke*, two vols (Mainz 1997 onwards). Original in English 1980.

Bach-Handbuch, ed Konrad Küster (Stuttgart and Weimar 1999): a reference work covering all questions on the present state of research.

The Cambridge Companion to Bach, ed by John Butt, (Cambridge 1997): insights and research by some of the most distinguished Bach scholars.

Bachs Otbestermusic. Ein Handbuch, ed Siegbert Raupe and P Sackmann, (Kassel 2000). *Bas Bachlexikon*, ed Michael Mienemann (London 2000).

GENERAL ACCOUNTS AND ILLUSTRATED BIOGRAPHIES

Johann Nikolaus Forkel, *Über Johann Sebastian Bachs Leben, Kunst und Kunstwerke* (Leipzig 1802), also published in various facsimile editions and reprints: the first account of Bach's life and work in book form after the *Obituary* (which appeared in 1754), partly based on the accounts of Bach's sons, partly creating legends even at this early date and setting Bach up as a national hero. English version 1820.

Philipp Spitta, *Johann Sebastian Bach*, two vols (Leipzig 1873 and 1880; photomechanical reprint of the 4th edn, Wiesbaden 1964): 'The Spitta' is one of the great musical biographies of the 19th and early 20th centuries, together with Friedrich Chrysander's biography of Handel, Ferdinand Pohl's of Haydn, Otto Jahn's of Mozart, Carl Glasenapp's of Wagner and Max Kalbeck's of Brahms. Still not superseded in that capacity, the work is now mainly of documentary value. English version 1884–5.

Albert Schweitzer, *J. S. Bach* (Leipzig 1908 and after): Schweitzer, although not strictly speaking a Bach scholar, laid the foundations for an aesthetic of Bach in a work of remarkably high quality, thus considerably extending the more historical work of Spitta. English version 1911.

Barbara Schwendowius and Wolfgang Dömling (eds), *J. S. Bach. Zeit – Leben – Wirken* (Kassel 1976).

Werner Felix, *J. S. Bach* (Leipzig 1984).

Hellmut Kühn, *J. S. Bach. Musik an der Wende* (Berlin 1984).

Martin Petzoldt and Joachim Petri, *J. S. Bach. Ehre sei dir Gott gesungen* (Berlin 1988): pictures and texts on Bach's life as a Christian and his work for the Church.

Christoph Wolff et al, *Die Bachfamilie* (Weimar and Stuttgart 1993) (The New Grove. *The Great Composers*): a more recent work on the many members of the Bach family. Original English version 1980.

Werner Breig, article on 'Bach' in *Die Musik in Geschichte und Gegenwart*, volume 1 of the part devoted to personalities (Kassel and Weimar 1999).

Martin Geck, Bach. *Leben und Werk* (Reinbek 2000): the latest general account. English version New York forthcoming.

INTRODUCTIONS TO THE WORKS IN PAPERBACK

Martin Geck, *J. S. Bach. Weihnachts-Oratorium* (Munich 1967).

Walter Blankenburg, *Einführung in Bachs h-moll-Messe* (3rd edn, Kassel 1974).

Walter Blankenburg, *Das Weihnachtsoratorium von J. S. Bach* (Kassel 1982).

Hans-Heinrich Eggebrecht: *Bachs Kunst der Fuge. Erscheinung und Deutung* (Munich and Zurich 1984).

Alfred Dürr, *Die Johannes-Passion von J. S. Bach* (Kassel 1988). English version 2000.

Emil Platen, *Die Matthäuspassion von J. S. Bach* (Kassel 1991).

Peter Schleuning, *Die Kunst der Fuge von J. S. Bach. Ideologien – Entstehung – Analyse* (Kassel 1993).

Alfred Dürr, *J. S. Bach. Das Wohltemperierte Klavier* (Kassel 1998).

Other monographs published in the *Meisterwerke der Musik* series by Wilhelm Fink Verlag, Munich.

WORKS USED FOR THE ENGLISH EDITION

Hans T David and Arthur Mendel (eds), *The Bach Reader* (revised edn, New York and London 1972).

Christoph Wolff, *Bach, Essays on His Life and Music* (Cambridge (Mass) 1993).

Christoph Wolff, *Johann Sebastian Bach, The Learned Musician* (New York and Oxford 2001).

Picture Sources

The author and publishers wish to express their thanks to the following sources of illustrative material and/or permission to reproduce it. They will make proper acknowledgements in future editions in the event that any omissions have occurred.

Ann Ronan Picture Library: pp. 38, 54, 77, 80, 118, 130, 141, 144; Bach Church, Arnstadt, photo Reinhold: p. 21; Bach House, Eisenach: pp. 3, 4, 5, 8, 17, 48; Bach Memorial, Köthen: p. 49; Michael Behns, Lüneburg: p. 19; Goethe Museum, Weimar: p. 25; Heinz Morgenstern, Leipzig: p. 67; Lebrecht Music Collection: pp. 6, 12, 15, 38, 66, 106; State Gallery, Leipzig: pp. 72, 74, 80, 92, 96, 120, 141; State Gallery, Maritzburg © Horst Fechner: p. 80. Topham Picturepoint: pp. iii, xiii, 130; Weimar Art Collection, photo Roland Dreßler: p. 36.

Index

126–7; growing privacy, 127; blindness, death and funeral, 128–9; faith and the Bible, 129, 143, 144; portraits, 130 WORKS: *Actus tragicus*, 24; *Das alte Jahr vergangen ist*, 111; *An Wasserflüssen Babylon*, 53; *Angenehmes Wiederau*, 117; *Art of Fugue (Die Kunst der Fuge)*, 30, 67, 107, 117, 121–2, 125–6, 128, 133–5, 136–7, 143; *Ascension Oratorio*, 138; *Auf! suss-entzückende Gewalt*, 138 *Aus der Tiefen rufe ich*, 24; B major partita BWV 825, 106; *B-minor Mass*, 46, 92, 108, 109, 117, 126, 132, 137–8, 142; *Bist du bei mir*, 108; *Brandenburg Concerti*, 50, 55, 56, 57, 59–62, 89, 103, 104; canon BWV 1073, 125; canon BWV 1076, 125; *Canon Per Augmentationem in contrario Motu*, 117; *Canonical Variations on the Christmas Hymn: Vom Himmel hoch da komm ich her*, 125, 134–5; Cantata No. 84, 28; cantata BWV 21, 55; cantata BWV 205, 85; cantata BWV 249a, 85; *Capriccio* BWV 992, 24; Catechism chorales, 107, 120, 122; *Christ Lag in Todesbanden*, 23; *Christmas Oratorio*, 97, 110, 114, 116–17; *Chromatic Fantasia*, 56, 64, 65; *Coffee Cantata*, 105, 142; concerti BWV 1052–1058, 104; concerto for three violins BWV 1064R, 57; *Dispute Between Phoebus and Pan*, 105; *Dorian Toccata*, 40; 'double' violin concerto BWV 1043, 57; *Du wahrer Gott und Davids Sohn*, 76; *Durchlauchster Leopold*, 56; 'Eighteen Chorales' BWV 651–668, 32; *Die Elenden sollen essen*, 81, 85, 86–9; English Suites, 64; *Es lebe der König, der Vater im Lande*, 126; Fantasia in C minor BWV Anh II, 45, 23; *Fantasia and Fugue in G minor* BWV 542, 55; flute sonatas BWV 1030 and 1032, 62, 104–5, 117; flute sonata BWV 1035, 63; four duets BWV 802–805, 107; French overture BWV 831, 107; French Suites, 64; funeral cantata *Klagt Kinder, klagt es aller Welt*, 49, 84; *Fürchte dich nicht, ich bin bei dir*, 91; *Der Geist hilft unser Schwachheit auf*, 91; *Geschwinde, ihr wirbelnden Winde*, 127; *Gleich wie der Regen und Schnee vom Himmel föllt*, 144; Goldberg Variations, 107, 108, 110, 112, 117, 121, 122, 134, 143; *Gott ist mein König*, 17, 24; *Herkules auf dem Scheidewege*, 114; *Der Herr denket an uns*, 23; *Herr Jesu Christ, dich zu uns wend*, 14; *Himmelskönig, sie*

willkommen, 34, 40; *Inventions* and *Sinfonias*, 64, 65, 67, 111; *Italian Concerto*, xi, 107, 110; *Jagdkantate*, 33, 60; *Jesu deine Passion*, 34; *Jesu, meine Freunde*, 65, 91–2; keyboard partite in A minor BWV 827, 82; keyboard partite in E minor BWV 830, 82; *Kinderlied auf die Weihnacht Christi*, 135; *Klavierbüchlein*, 41, 65, 108; *Klavierübung*, 74, 106–7, 110–12, 120–21, 142; *Komm, Jesu, komm*, 91; *Magnificat*, 92; *Missa Brevis*, 98–9; *Musical Offering*, 62, 67, 117, 124, 133–5; *Nach dir, Herr, verlanget mich*, 23; *Nun komm, der Heiden Heiland*, 35, 40; oboe d'amore concerto BWV 1055a, 57; oboe and violin concerto BWV 1060, 57; organ chorales BWV 651–668, 122; organ sonatas BWV 525–530, 42, 104; organ trios BWV 645–650, 125; *Orgelbüchlein*, 29, 30–32, 33, 110–11; 'overtures' BWV 1066–1069, 62, 103; partite BWV 1013, 63; Passion (BC D 1), 35; *Peasant Cantata*, 105, 110, 117, 142; *Piano Practice*, 107; Prelude and Fugue in C major BWV 531, 22; *Preise dein Glücke, gesegnetes Sachsen*, 101, 126; Prelude in D major BWV 874, 117; Prelude and Fugue BWV 552, 107; *St John Passion*, 35, 78–9, 92–3, 144; *St Luke Passion*, 93; *St Mark Passion*, 93; *St Matthew Passion*, 49, 78–9, 84–5, 92–5, 100, 137, 139; *Schübler Chorales*, 42; *Singet dem Herrn ein neues Lied*, 37, 91; *So lasset uns gehen in Salem der Freuden*, 34, 36; sonatas and partitas for solo violin BWV 1001–1006, 43, 63; suites for solo cello BWV 1007–1012, 43, 63; Toccata in C major BWV 564, 40; Toccata in D minor BWV 565, 22; *Tombeau* BWV 198, 100; *Tönet, ihr Pauken! Erschallet, Trompeten!*, 114, 116; *Vater unser in Himmelreich*, 111; viola da gamba sonatas BWV 1027–1029, 63, 104–5; violin concerto in A minor BWV 1041, 57, 104; violin concerto in E major BWV 1042, 57, 104; violin concerto BWV 1052a; violin concerto 1056a, 57; violin partita in D minor BWV 1004, 64; violin sonatas BWV 1014–1019, 63; *Wachtet! Betet! Betet! Wachet!*, 114; *Weinen, Klagen, Sorgen, Zagen*, 35, 46; *Well-tempered Clavier*, 16, 39, 47, 64–9, 107, 110, 117, 122, 132, 146; *Wenn wir im höchsten Nöten sind*, 128; *Wer nur den lieben Gott lässt*